CW00541880

ONE WOMAN'S WAR

AND PEACE

SHARON BOWN grew up in Tasmania, where she completed her Bachelor of Nursing and commenced work as a Registered Nurse. Dissatisfied with her comfortable life, in 1999 she left home to join the Royal Australian Air Force as a Nursing Officer. Over her sixteen-year military career, she served at multiple locations throughout Australia and overseas, including a position of sub-unit command in Townsville and operational command in Afghanistan.

Sharon is a Member of the Council of the Australian War Memorial, and is a passionate advocate for Australia's military nurses and for military and veterans' health. She is highly sought after to speak of the unique experiences of her service career. The original manuscript for this, her first book, was awarded First Prize in the Literature division of the 2016 Air Force Heritage Awards. Sharon lives in Townsville with her husband, who is an Army Officer, and their two sons.

ONE WOMAN'S WAR

AND PEACE

A NURSE'S JOURNEY IN THE ROYAL AUSTRALIAN AIR FORCE

Wing Commander
Sharon Bown (Ret'd)

An HOURGLASS book
An imprint of Exisle Publishing Pty Ltd

First published 2016

Exisle Publishing Pty Ltd
'Moonrising', Narone Creek Road, Wollombi, NSW 2325, Australia
P.O. Box 60–490, Titirangi, Auckland 0642, New Zealand
www.exislepublishing.com

Copyright © 2016 in text: Sharon Bown

Sharon Bown asserts the moral right to be identified as the author of this work.

All rights reserved. Except for short extracts for the purpose of review, no part of this book may be reproduced, stored in a retrieval system or transmitted in any form or by any means, whether electronic, mechanical, photocopying, recording or otherwise, without prior written permission from the publisher.

A CiP record for this book is available from the National Library of Australia.

ISBN 978 1 925335 31 6

Cover photographs of the author by Conway Bown
Designed by Nick Turzynski of redinc. book design
Maps by Nick Turzynski of redinc. book design
Typeset in Bembo 12/17
Printed in China

This book uses paper sourced under ISO 14001 guidelines from well−managed forests and other controlled sources.

10 9 8 7 6 5 4 3 2 1

Disclaimer
While this book is intended as a general information resource and all care has been taken in compiling the contents, neither the author nor the publisher and their distributors can be held responsible for any loss, claim or action that may arise from reliance on information contained in this book.

For my husband Conway, and our precious boys,
Tiberius and Austin

For the men, women and families dedicated to the
service of Australia.

CONTENTS

FOREWORD

'I have worn their blood. So many of us have worn their blood.'

Two sentences with immense power and resonance. They were quietly spoken in pre-dawn darkness to thousands of Australians assembled at the Australian War Memorial for Anzac Day 2014. With quiet, awkward humility and abiding reverence they were the words of Sharon Bown. Behind her, onto the front of the Memorial were being projected the images of the men killed in Afghanistan whose blood she had 'worn'.

None of us present will ever forget the power of the moment.

Proudly wearing her Royal Australian Air Force uniform for the last time, more than anyone else she conveyed in that one speech all that military service represents. She conveyed the courage and price paid by those who wear the uniform of our three services in the protection of our nation and its values. She also laid bare her own humanity and that of those whom she treated leading a critical care team in Afghanistan.

Courage comes in many forms — physical, moral and emotional. *One Woman's War and Peace* manifests all three. This is Sharon Bown's remarkable story.

Pulled from the wreck of a UN Bell helicopter in East Timor, soaked in aviation fuel with crushed vertebrae and a broken jaw, this RAAF nurse was determined to return to work as soon as she could. Carrying both the physical and psychological pain of this near-death experience, twice in 2004, she returned to work as soon as she could. She helped choose the medical team to assist in Nias after the 2005 tsunami. Then she endured the agony of learning some of those closest to her whom she had selected had been killed in the Sea King helicopter tragedy. She would deploy to Bali after the second bombing in 2005 to provide expert nursing care. She lost and found love, suffered the death of her mother and then, whilst working as my Aide-de-Camp when Defence Minister, her police officer father was shot on duty.

Sharon Bown was determined that these major life events — despite her post-traumatic stress — would make her stronger. And they did. She writes that being 'broken' gave her the 'opportunity for growth' and to be 'more complete' than she had been. In then exploring the extent of her capabilities, she is testament to the truism that it is not what happens in life that determines its value, but how you deal with it.

The operating theatre in which Sharon worked in Afghanistan and her description of it says much about the Australian character. The Australian Special Forces had presented her team with an Australian flag. She hung it on the wall inside the operating theatre. It would be the last thing these men would see when they went under and the first thing they would see when they awoke.

The most poignant description of her remarkable work there, however, is that of an eight-year-old Afghan boy shot in his home by a stray bullet, curled up as he slept. Describing it as her 'darkest hour', she writes:

We lost a child. A child who cried for someone or something in his mother tongue as we put him to sleep for surgery. A child who cried to a room full of strangers who could not understand his pleas.

It has taken a great deal of courage to live the life she has in the uniform of the Royal Australian Air Force. But perhaps it has taken more courage for Sharon Bown to tell it.

In doing so, she has told the stories of all those remarkable men and women who serve, each in their own way — for us. She gives us a unique insight into the cost of that service and the price paid not only by those in the uniform, but those who love and support them.

There are many books on 'leadership' and an entire industry of people purporting to teach it.

Leadership can't be taught, but it can be learned. It can be absorbed through reflection on the lives and leadership experiences of others. Some lead from position, others from principle. Sharon Bown has done both.

Character derives from the Greek word meaning 'the impression left in wax by a stone, seal ring'. It is informed by values — worthwhile intrinsic virtues. Above rank, influence, wealth and everything else stands character.

One Woman's War and Peace is a story about character and leadership. One woman and the lives she has touched are an inspirational testament to power of character. Wing Commander Sharon Bown (Ret'd) has done the Royal Australian Air Force and the nation it serves proud.

Hon Dr Brendan Nelson AO
Director, Australian War Memorial

PREFACE

The following story is an account of events drawn from the memory of a single person: mine. Memories of experiences and life events are as specific as they are personal to those involved. Events evoke different reactions, different emotions and hence completely different viewpoints and memories for each individual. The following story is my story. It is my account of my life experience. I acknowledge that I did not live through these events alone, but I hold dear the way in which I survived them as an individual, and the way in which my life has altered as a result.

With great pride, I concede that my story defines me and my family as collateral damage of the proud and honourable mission of the Australian Defence Force: to defend Australia and its national interests. I am not bitter, nor do I regret the sacrifices I have made in the service of my country. I understood the risks involved at every stage of my service career and I have been free to choose to proceed or withdraw at any time. I am accountable for my choices and I believe it is this personal acknowledgement, made during the course of my recovery, that has enabled me to prevail as a survivor of my service and not a victim. I acknowledge that not all survivors are free to make such choices, nor are they always supported to do so. In the service of Australia, the unintended casualties that result do not only occur in the Australian Defence Force, but also within Australia's emergency services, including police, fire, ambulance and the state emergency service.

I hope that in sharing my story there may be a greater acknowledgement and acceptance of these casualties, which result from the continued protection of our unique and precious way of life. While we must always continue to commemorate and honour those who have died in the service of Australia, we must never forget those who have willingly paid the penultimate sacrifice. Indebted to their sacrifice, may we, at the very least, do them no further harm.

I would like to express my thanks to a number of people.

To my husband Conway for his continued encouragement for me to document my story and for his invaluable suggestions, editing and graphic design. Without his insistence that my story should be told, this publication would have only ever existed on my bucket list. I reserve the right to continue to shake my head at his constant cajoling.

To my parents and grandparents, who have always believed that I would make the right decisions in life and who have ultimately provided me with the greatest example of living life in the service of others.

To Doug and Cate Rawlinson, better friends you would rarely find. Through my trials and tribulations, they have always been there.

To my good friend Wing Commander Lara Gunn. I thank her for her friendship, counsel and comradeship. Her presence throughout my Air Force career, from our first, faltering steps at Officer Training School until now as I embark upon my civilian life, has been of great comfort.

To Squadron Leader Kay Wiseman, my friend, my confidante, the quiet presence throughout my journey who has taught me how to be stronger and faster than I could have ever imagined I would be.

To Air Commodore Michael Paterson DSM, my mentor and friend, without whose wise counsel and support I may not have always been able to overcome the hurdles of my Air Force career.

To the Hon Dr Brendan Nelson AO, for his unfaltering belief in the value of telling the stories of the men, women and families of the Australian Defence Force. Mine is just one of many.

To Gabriela Leite-Soares, my *alin feto* Gabi, a shining example of the possibilities of the remarkable youth of Timor Leste.

To all that have supported me along my journey and to those who believed that my story needed to be told. Thank you to AUSMTF2, Melissa Bingley, Sharon Boobyer, Colonel Ross Bradford, Sergeant Maria Brown, Group Captain Gregor Bruce, Captain Gemma Coenen, Dr Janice Cudmore, Dr Greg Day, Wing Commander Michel and Paul Devine, Squadron Leader Alexander 'Sandy' Donald, Wing Commander Nicole dos Santos, Major General Anthony Fraser CSC, Dr Stephen Frederickson, Wing Commander Doug Gow (Retd), Group Captain Bill Griggs, Dr John Groemer, Jo Harding, Jasmine Healy-Pagan, Group Captain Annette Holian, Air Chief Marshal Sir Angus Houston AK, AFC (Ret'd), Greg Jack, Belinda Johnson, Cherrie Johnston, Squadron Leader Karen Knewstub, Dr Martha Landman, Dr Michael Likely, Helen Ross, Group Captain David Scott, Air Vice Marshal Tracy Smart AM, Kath Thomas, Christine Upchurch-Neal, Dr Matthew Voltz, Wing Commander Ross Wadsworth (Retd), Group Captain Michele Walker, Dr Patrick Weinrauch, Colin and Nat Young, and to the late Roy and Jan Paine.

Lastly, I am indebted to the Royal Australian Air Force — my military family and an organization that took me in, trained me and allowed me to meet so many outstanding people and experience the wide range of life events that have shaped me. Some experiences were horrific, some disappointing, but for the most part they were rich and rewarding. The motto of the Royal Australian Air Force is *Per ardua ad astra*, which translates as 'Through adversity to the stars'. I may have struggled through adversity to reach the stars, but the struggle was well worth the effort and for any reader thinking of a career in the military, I hope this story encourages you to do so.

Sharon Bown
Wing Commander (Ret'd)
Townsville, Queensland, 2016

PROLOGUE

Lying face down in the mud I felt pain searing through my body. Mere seconds before I had been perched 3 metres above the ground, balanced precariously on a crashed Bell 212 helicopter, stuck rigid, and in excruciating pain. Another desperate survivor had pushed against my broken back and toppled me forward, freeing me from the wreckage. But there was an agonizing price to pay. I landed in the mud, the raw edges of my shattered bones grinding against shattered bone. I struggled to cope with such acute physical pain, unlike anything I had ever known, and I could hear the harrowing scream of the helicopter's engines dying behind me. My fuel-soaked flying suit clung to my skin and I knew I was still in extremely serious danger.

Dazed, I struggled to lift my head from the mud. My flying helmet was heavy and my neck muscles began to constrict in response to the life-threatening jolt they had endured moments before. Through the relentless tropical rain, the scene that lay before me only intensified my fear: a modest mountain village, a concerned yet humble people, and an impoverished country. As the helicopter had plummeted towards the trees I had made my final farewells to those I loved and accepted that today would be the day I would die. I didn't. But at a cost. The pain of survival seemed unbearable, even compared to an impending death.

'I don't want to do this. This can't be happening,' I thought.

I rested my head upon the earth and closed my eyes.

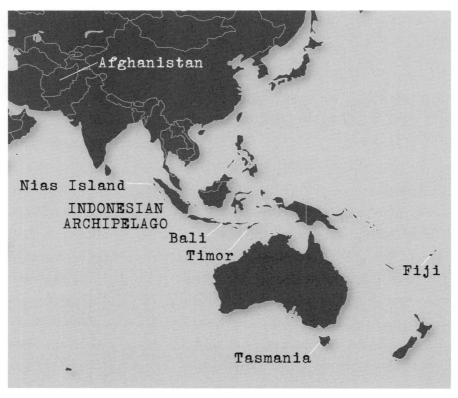

Australia's Sphere of Interest

Australia's security relies on its Sphere of Influence and Sphere of Interest being stable. Any instability in the region is of great concern to the Australian Government, and the Australian Defence Force — as an instrument of Government foreign policy — will often find itself deployed to areas within the region.

CHAPTER 1

OFFICER TRAINING SCHOOL

January 1999

Australian military service had always interested me. Possessing a fairly conservative nature, though, I never thought I would be suited to the nomadic and potentially dangerous lifestyle of the Australian military. At high school I listened eagerly to the recruiters as they explained the financial benefits of having the Australian Defence Force, the ADF, fund your university degree. I daydreamed about serving my country in the long-revered tradition of the ANZACs but, alas, at seventeen years of age I did not yet have the spirit of adventure, or the courage that had spurred those fine young Australians into action some 75 years earlier.

I was the third of four daughters born to happily married parents. My father was a police officer and my mother stayed at home to care for us until my later primary school years, when she returned to work

RAAF Bases mentioned

as a nursing aide caring for the elderly and infirm. We had a humble and happy childhood and my parents worked hard to give us every opportunity they could afford.

Unlike many female students of my generation I loved science and math and the physicality of team sports, such as hockey and netball. So it might have seemed out of character for me to pursue nursing, a career in the female-dominated 'helping' profession. But I wanted to make a difference in the lives of others and I watched in awe as my mother showed how compassionately this could be done. In choosing nursing, I became the first person in my family to attend university. By the age of

23 I had completed my Bachelor of Nursing and was living a comfortable life in Tasmania with my boyfriend of five years.

Ironically, given my comfortable existence, my eventual decision to join the Royal Australian Air Force, the RAAF, arose from the very conservatism that had earlier held me back. I had been working as a Registered Nurse for three years and was enjoying the challenge of perioperative work in the operating theatre — providing nursing care to patients before, during and immediately after surgery. I loved the nursing specialty I had chosen yet began to feel that, even though I was still a very junior clinician, I already possessed the knowledge, skills and experience that could assist those less fortunate than myself. I also realized that I was working in the hospital where I had been born and might end up being groomed to take over from my baby boomer colleagues. So I started to look for adventure.

At work I listened to the plastic surgeons and some of the more senior nurses talk of their humanitarian work overseas and I felt that it would be many years before I would be ready to accompany such an elite team. At the same time, I sensed a growing urge within me to provide humanitarian assistance to those in need, to travel overseas and discover other cultures, and to find an existence so removed from my own that I would fully appreciate the world into which chance had delivered me. I had witnessed the great Ethiopian famine of 1984 from the comfort of my parent's living room through the safety of a colour TV screen and, like so many other Australian children, my mother had frequently threatened to send my uneaten dinner to the starving children in China. Superficially, I knew that there was suffering in the world but I wanted to experience a greater depth of life and with an intensity that would not disappear with the switch of a channel or be diluted by another unwanted mouthful of cabbage.

It was the Air Force that would become my passage to this dramatically different world and bring me close to the immense suffering of others. It also taught me something else: the mostly unseen sacrifice of those who serve their country.

I was proud to have an opportunity to serve my country, to have the skills and experience to do so and a level of health and fitness such a position demanded. Asked why I chose the Air Force and not the Navy or Army, I would jokingly reply that my favourite colour was blue. Indeed, my favourite colour is blue, but that was certainly not why I sought to join the Air Force over the other services. I suffer from motion sickness at sea so I was not keen on spending extended periods of time working aboard a ship in the Navy and, as my family had enjoyed at least four weeks of each year camping, I was not attracted to the amount of time Army Nursing Officers spent under canvas in the field. I was, though, drawn to the aeromedical evacuation role of the Air Force Nursing Officer.

The Air Force not only offered me the opportunity for defence service but a unique and exciting opportunity to learn a type of nursing new to me; one that enabled the rapid delivery of healthcare to those in need. The prospect of flying into places to get patients out and nursing them in the back of an aircraft provided me a great adrenaline rush and sparked my interest in the role. With a quick phone call and a follow-up visit to the Defence Force Recruiting offices in Hobart, I was past the first hurdle, promptly recruited into the Air Force, and scheduled to undertake officer training.

My first memories of Officer Training School (OTS) were of a not-so-brave, young civilian nurse standing on the edge of an oval at RAAF Base Williams (Point Cook) in Victoria. Here I was within the boundary of the oldest continuous serving military airfield in the world and readying to join the great tradition of Air Force Officers who had already had the privilege to serve within its grounds. That was all very well, but right then I was hoping that no one would see the tears in my eyes or hear the quiver in my voice as I attempted to gulp back the emotional lump in my throat and reassure my parents and boyfriend that I had arrived safely and that I was okay.

I saw no need to tell them that I had fallen asleep in the taxi from the airport, blindly trusting a driver who, in broken English, had thrust a street directory at me and told me that I would have to show him where to go. The small-town, timid Tasmanian girl who had absolutely no idea of where she was going, in any sense, had set out on her adventure and was feeling a sense of fear. I felt so far outside my comfort zone and far from my family, my friends and my boyfriend. My life back in Tasmania had been so comfortable that I had an overwhelming desire to call another taxi and board a flight back home. I quickly reminded myself, though, that if my new sense of isolation, trepidation and doubt were part of the adventure I had sought, it was meant to be.

Officer training was challenging but it was not terrifying. It would turn out to be one of the most enjoyable times of my life, helping me evolve from a shy girl into a confident woman prepared for adventure and rewarding me with friends and colleagues to see out a career and maybe even a lifetime.

On my first day of training, as we gathered as a group outside the accommodation block, a male voice barked from out of nowhere, instructing us to 'form up'. Everyone around me moved almost instantly to stand in neat rows on the edge of the roadway. I, not having any idea what form up meant, naively followed and stood among them. It was, of course, a very military thing to do but to me it seemed odd as we had not yet been issued uniforms and were still in an array of civilian clothes.

Despite our military formation, the individuality of our group was evident with its mix of gender, race and physical attributes; within 24 hours, that individuality would be less obvious when we would proudly adopt the uniform of the Royal Australian Air Force. While form up seemed easy enough, the authoritative voice then shouted even more commands that were foreign to me: 'Attention', 'Left turn',

'By the right', 'Quick march'. All of this spurred the otherwise neatly formed group around me to change direction and begin walking, arms swinging and in perfect time with each other. They were marching; I, like some weak member of the herd, was flailing around in their midst, one out-of-step stride behind, doing my utmost to simply keep up. I suddenly realized that I had a great deal more to learn than I might ever have expected.

I continued to feel like a fish out of water for the first few weeks of training, but my colleagues were quick to assist. The Directing Staff (DS) were even quicker in their own way, presenting themselves as the common enemy, espousing the one-in-all-in philosophy that also translated as 'one screws up, all will suffer'. I learned to do many things with precision: to march, to iron, to tie my hair in a bun. I soon understood that there was never any reason to have my hands in my pockets, and that showering quickly was not only a necessary part of what some might call the 'bastardisation' process, it also saved on making too much mess that I would later be obliged to clean up.

I could iron my bedclothes while they remained on the bed and clean my room so it appeared no one lived there. There were a few colleagues who at the end of the course had not once slept in their bed for fear of having to make it again. A chaplain on the course ahead of me described the moment when he knew officer training had changed him. Standing at attention at the end of his bed awaiting the critical assessment of his DS, he spotted a dead cockroach on the floor. The chaplain pounced on it, sweeping it up in an instant to secret it away in his uniform pocket before the DS inspection would reveal him to be a poor example of an Air Force Officer. As he stood at attention, cockroach securely hidden from sight, he asked himself, 'Where else in the world would I shove a dead cockroach into my pocket?'

I was far from being considered for the Officer Qualities Award at the conclusion of training, but that was okay by me. I worked hard to be what was known as the 'grey man', the person who blended into the group, not at all drawing any attention to themself. More notable than these 'military achievements', it was during officer training that I gained my career-long nickname of 'Coops', from my maiden name Cooper; I made the most of my grey man status to become incredibly good at a murder party card game known as Mafia; and I became renowned for the head shake. Apparently when I disapprove of anything, I shake my head, something I learned about only from living and working with the same group of people for fifteen weeks.

I was pleased to have kept and, indeed, gained some personal traits, despite having worked so hard to adapt to the stringent standards of dress and bearing required of a military officer. For women, long hair was to be secured in a bun and short hair cut above the collar and secured neatly behind the ears. Hair was required to be of a natural colour and make-up neutral. Fingernails were to be short and not coloured. The only jewellery allowed was one small stud per ear, a plain wristwatch and no more than two rings per hand.

As the daughter of a police sergeant, the structured and certain way of life in the Air Force was not a surprise for me and I was good at following rules. Also, my nursing career had taught me a lot about dress standards, time management and working within a team. I could see some of the others were finding the transition a little harder, struggling to get out of bed on time and to dress themselves to the required standard. This was the time when we learned to care for each other. Those with previous military experience helped those of us with none and we quickly learned teamwork, appreciating that it was benefiting us all.

As the course progressed, I began to relax a little and enjoy myself more. I had begun to make friends, including fellow Tasmanian Lara Gunn. She was diminutive but driven and had entered the Air Force as a pharmacist. To look at her, one would not expect that she would choose the life of an ADF officer, but both of us were in it together: two Tasmanian girls on their big adventure as the Air Force tried to mould us into something they could use. Lara and I would become firm friends.

The training ranged from academic studies of subjects, such as air power, Defence Force discipline, security and Defence writing, to activities and field exercises designed to demonstrate and assess leadership, teamwork, problem-solving and military skills. I learned to 'play the game', realizing that while OTS was providing me with the knowledge, skills and experience required of an Air Force Officer, it was also a test of my hardiness and resilience, the essentials for my future career.

On my 24th birthday I got the clearest sign yet of what I had signed myself up for. We had by this time relocated or, as I would now say, 'deployed' to RAAF Base East Sale in Gippsland, eastern Victoria, to carry out a ground defence exercise. It can get very cold around East Sale and while inspecting the base's Air Force Health Centre we were shown the hypothermia bed, there to treat trainee officers who succumbed to numbing cold while undertaking the very sort of ground force exercise awaiting us. Despite having grown up in chilly Tasmania this was not an encouraging sight.

As trainee defenders of the nation we were to set-up a defensive posture around a designated 'key point' or asset that was to be protected. Among many other things, this necessitated that at all times we carried the ADF standard issue service rifle, the F88 AUSteyr. If you left your rifle behind it was quickly replaced with a heavy steel fence post or stake that was very awkward to carry. Such punishment was humiliating and irritating enough to ensure you never forgot your rifle. Adding some realism to the situation, we were issued with blank ammunition and rigorously followed weapons handling techniques. Any mistake in weapon handling could result in an accidental discharge of the weapon, which would lead to the perpetrator being charged and prosecuted under the Defence Force Discipline Act.

While this type of ground defence responsibility would not normally fall to a Nursing Officer, it was vital that all Air Force Officers were cognizant of the process so they were able to carry out the basics in a conflict zone. I am still grateful for the time spent in training with the F88, as throughout my career, I would be armed on overseas operations for a combined total of twelve months — a laughable achievement for a soldier perhaps, but a contradiction in terms for a healthcare professional trained to preserve life, not take it.

Our training was now well and truly out in the field. We dug weapons pits — two-man trenches from which to fire our weapons — around the perimeter of a key point and from which we could adopt an 'outward-looking defensive posture'. We slept immediately behind our weapon's pit so that in the event of potential attack we could easily jump into them and defend our position from opposing forces — the 'bad guys'.

As eager young officer trainees, our attempts to fulfil this responsibility were often more humorous than effective. At East Sale, we 'stood-to' to protect the key point from a suspicious-looking kangaroo advancing on our position, and at Puckapunyal, the Australian Army's home to the School of Armour, where mud is mud in summer and frozen in winter, a fellow officer became spooked when he became aware of a Leopard tank in our vicinity, calling us all to stand-to and man our defensive positions. I'm sure that Army soldiers at Puckapunyal felt reassured knowing that their Air Force counterparts were keeping their base safe from Australia's very own tanks! My favourite memory is of two officers who slept through a middle-of-the-night attack by the 'enemy' because one successfully convinced the other that he must be hearing things. Some might think that the firing of weapons is a convincing enough sound.

Had I been back in Tasmania in my former life on my 24th birthday I might have taken the day off and treated myself to a long and peaceful sleep in and later gone out to dinner and drinks with my friends. But on this birthday, I was awoken suddenly by the very convincing sound of simulated mortar fire. It was bitterly cold and we were sleeping out in the open, on the ground behind our weapons pit. In order to keep myself as warm as possible I had pulled the drawstring of my sleeping bag hood as tight as possible and then tied it securely. There was just enough room for my nose and mouth to draw in fresh air. Having tied the hood when I was awake the night before, I had not considered having to undo it when not quite so awake.

As the mortar fire 'rained down', simulated by the frightening and annoying explosives known as whizz-bangs (owing to their unique sound), I jumped up to take shelter in my weapons pit. Trapped in my sleeping bag and in blind panic, I could not undo the knot. I writhed and wriggled around on the ground like an epileptic caterpillar until I eventually broke free from my cocoon, not-so-much a beautiful butterfly but more a dishevelled and confused officer cadet, and dived into the hole in the ground in front of me. Thank goodness for the dim dawn light that protected me from utter embarrassment. There, in the subzero cold and peering out over the dirt edge, rifle poised and ready with small arms and mortar fire sounding around me, I shook my head and muttered to myself, 'Happy Birthday, Sharon. What the hell are you doing?!'

The day brought no further incident but it was to end with a treat. Our Ground Defence Officer announced it was my birthday and I was allowed a single phone call. I just had to decide if my family or my boyfriend should be the recipient of this valued gift. The Directing Staff had hearts after all. I took the phone and was looking for somewhere quiet to phone my boyfriend as it would be nice to hear his voice and listen to some tales of the life I had left behind. But before I could disappear a gruff announcement burst forth: 'Get used to it, Cooper, this will be the first of many birthdays away from home for you.' What a cheery thought. But it was indeed an accurate one as a year later I was on a military operation working alongside Egyptians, Singaporeans and Portuguese. On my 25th birthday, I would awake to a plaintive Muslim call to prayer. We were soon to enter the new millennium and I would be in Dili, East Timor.

CHAPTER 2

DEPLOYMENT TO EAST TIMOR

February 2000

All freshly minted Nursing Officers were assigned to one of the two larger Air Force hospitals, where there were more staff to help us in our transition into military nursing. By this time, I was well into the jargon and knew these two bigger hospitals at Laverton in Victoria near Point Cook and at Richmond on the north-western edge of the Sydney sprawl by their ADF titles: No. 6 Hospital, Laverton, and No. 3 Hospital, Richmond. I requested a posting to 3 Hospital. I was still feeling a little homesick and knew that, if I was going to make a good go of my new venture, I needed to put some distance between myself and Hobart, and resist racing back home each weekend.

I had enjoyed Officer Training School and made some great friends but now I was leaving most of them behind as we went our separate ways across the country to our first postings. As I moved to RAAF Base Richmond, my boyfriend packed up his belongings in Hobart and followed me and my career to New South Wales. I arrived at 3 Hospital in May 1999 and, within four months, I watched with a mixture of apprehension and excitement as those around me were rapidly deployed to East Timor, or Timor-Leste as it is known in the local language, after the referendum for independence from Indonesia and the violence that followed. I was getting my first real look at the true potential of my new career. It was exciting to watch the situation unfold on the evening news and then to witness the behind-the-scenes work where I was stationed, as those around me readied for deployment. Men and women wearing the same uniform that I now proudly wore poured into East Timor on the peace enforcement operation to stabilize the country and protect its citizens.

The TV news showed Australian Army helicopters patrolling the skies over the capital of Dili, with soldiers sitting in the open doors, ready to leap out to chase militia. Warships of the Royal Australian Navy ferried troops and equipment to the island and the Air Force was working around the clock delivering food and aid to the people of East Timor. Within weeks I too was identified to be deployed on this military operation. No. 3 Hospital had been given the mission to take command of the United Nations Military Hospital in Dili in February 2000 and, having perioperative nursing skills, I would be a member of the theatre team within the hospital. I was being given the sort of assignment for which I had joined up.

It had been rare for Australian military personnel to be sent overseas since the end of the Vietnam War and yet here I was being handed an opportunity that many long-time service members had never been offered. There would have been some Nursing Officers around the country cursing me as a 'baby', in the service only 'since breakfast time', but already setting out on an adventure they would die for. Excited, I phoned my parents with the news. My family was still coming to terms with my decision to leave Tasmania to follow a military career and now I was letting them know I was being sent overseas.

My mother and I had often discussed what appeared to be a perfect plan regarding my foray into the Air Force. I told her I would be away for six months and she was very clear in her response: 'Well, Sharon, that's wonderful. You can go and do that and when you get back, you can come home.' In her mind I would have accomplished what I had set out to do and, having got that out of my system, I could come back to my family where she felt I belonged. My parents were so very proud of my commitment to military service and had always supported my choices, and there was a service history within the family.

In his early working life my father was a boilermaker, welder and had served for nine years as an Army Reservist with B Company of the 40th Battalion, Royal Tasmanian Regiment. He reached the rank of Sergeant and became the B Company Drill Sergeant before discharging to pursue a career as a Police Officer in the Tasmania Police force. His younger brother Peter had also served in the Army, including a tour of duty in Vietnam. My family was far from ignorant to the adverse affects of military service, yet they supported my decision. Perhaps it was their faith that I could look after myself, or an Army bias that believed Air Force Officers, and in particular Nursing Officers, were unlikely to ever see any real danger. During my career a cousin joined the Air Force and another cousin and a nephew joined the Army, with my sister Annette enduring a pain that many mothers describe as far greater than childbirth: watching her only son leave to go to war. All of them served proudly and returned home safely.

On Monday, 14 February 2000 — Valentine's Day — I left Australia for the first time. I never considered how profound this moment would be, to depart my homeland for a foreign shore in turmoil. I was about to be as far away from my home and my family as I had ever been, in the company of people I had only just met or had never met. I felt no threat to my personal safety and I had few preconceived ideas about East Timor. However, I was uncertain about how I would perform because as yet I didn't really know what my role in East Timor would involve.

The island of Timor lies 640 kilometres from Australia. It was colonized by the Portuguese in the sixteenth century and then partitioned with the Dutch in the nineteenth century. During the Second World War, the Japanese occupied the island and mounted bombing raids against the Australian mainland from Timor. The Timorese suffered at the hands of the Japanese and many were executed for helping Australian soldiers fighting there. After the war, the Dutch colonies in the west transitioned into the country of Indonesia, with the Portuguese retaining the eastern half. In 1975, Indonesia illegally annexed East Timor with much violence and bloodshed. Thousands died at the hands of Indonesia or through starvation. In 1999, after pressure from Australia, the United States and the United Nations, Indonesia agreed to allow a referendum to take place to determine if East Timor would gain independence or remain under its control. The referendum was overwhelmingly in favour of independence but the ensuing violence by the Indonesian-backed militia shocked the world. It was this series of events that led to the Australian-led military intervention in October 1999.

There was much that I needed to come to terms with about this deployment as I underwent the pre-deployment preparation and training. I was still learning how to be a Nursing Officer in the Air Force but was now very rapidly needing to learn how to perform this role outside Australia. One of the things that struck me immediately was the very great distinction between civilian and military nursing, with military nurses being required to move between mostly benign clinical settings and some of the worst trauma scenes in the world. I did at least know that I would be working in an operating theatre and that was within my comfort zone. I was returning to an aspect of working life that I had loved back home.

Just how fortunate I had been growing up in a country like Australia hit me as I stepped out onto the tarmac of the Dili airfield and took the

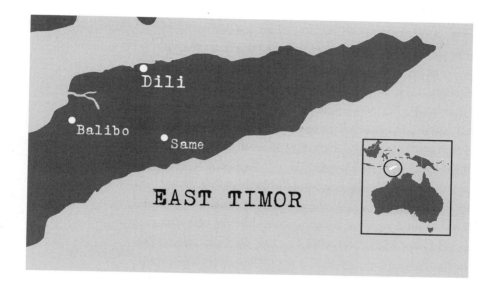

drive through the city's streets to the place that would serve as my home and place of work for at least six months: the United Nations Military hospital, which in true military fashion I would refer to as UNMILHOSP. I had seen the TV footage of East Timorese seeking refuge at the United Nations' compound after the referendum for independence, throwing their children over the barbed wire fences in the hope that they would be kept safe from the violence that ensued. What greeted us on that very first drive through Dili was a deserted and destroyed landscape.

Burned-out buildings lined the roads, which carried more military vehicles and armed personnel than they did locals. The very few locals we did see waved and cheered as we passed, apparently celebrating the presence of their saviours. The East Timorese were of a small and fine stature, their skin brown and their hair beautifully thick, dark and mostly curly, but what struck me were their smiles, particularly those of the children. Knowing the recent history of their trauma and the reason for our military intervention in their country, I was instantly taken by these faces that glowed with what I can only describe as happiness. Everything, from their clothing to their surrounding architecture, screamed destitution and hardship to me, yet their faces beamed with joy.

The air was thick with a smothering, hot humidity and a distinctive smell that in some areas was highlighted by wastewater or even sewage, and in others the tropical scent of the frangipani trees and fresh sea breeze. Before I had even arrived at my destination, East Timor was beginning to reveal itself as a country of contradictions. Traumatized people now seemed invigorated by the success of their independence vote and the promise of assistance and aid from the developed world, a world that until recently had seemed to have forgotten about them. Children who appeared to have nothing managed to find fun and games on the side of the road.

Eventually we caught our first glimpse of the hospital compound. The distinctive red roof of its main building resembled a citrus juicer, an impressive piece of local architecture that would of course become known to us as 'The Squeezer'. It was a place of great significance, as it had been the Dili Museum and later the site of the ballot count in the referendum. During the vote, because of the actions of anti-independence militias, United Nations Mission East Timor (UNAMET) decided that all ballot papers from all areas around East Timor would be mixed prior to being counted in a central location. This prevented the identification of pro-independence areas and thus reduced the chance of reprisals against them.

UNAMET had organized the referendum, held on 30 August 1999, which allowed the East Timorese to choose between autonomy within Indonesia or independence. Of the 99 per cent of the population who cast a vote, 78.5 per cent voted in favour of independence. Despite the clear majority, anti-independence militias set upon a violent and destructive rampage throughout East Timor, killing citizens and destroying buildings and infrastructure. It was this that led to the formation and deployment of the Australian-led UN peace enforcement, and then the peacekeeping force, International Force for East Timor, or more simply, INTERFET.

The Squeezer had largely survived the civil unrest and, following the election, the Australian Army's 1st Field Hospital transformed it and its adjacent buildings and grounds into a fit-for-purpose field hospital. Their mandate, in support of the INTERFET mission, was to provide healthcare to INTERFET personnel and to carry out eye, limb and lifesaving surgery for East Timorese locals. As INTERFET handed responsibility for peacekeeping operations over to the United Nations, our role would be to provide similar medical support to the UN mission and the UN peacekeeping force. We would retain the mandate to carry out eye, limb and lifesaving surgery for East Timorese locals.

We were fortunate to arrive at a well-established facility and gratefully expressed our appreciation for the hard work of our Army colleagues. But the Army were still staffing and operating the hospital so our needs would remain secondary to theirs until they returned home. Our living quarters were outside and at the rear of the hospital compound. We set-up our stretchers and mozzie domes inside the shell of a concrete building that had a dirt floor and no windowpanes and no doors in the doorframes. I had camped in worse conditions, and I knew the Diggers in the Army were doing it much harder. Despite the primitive accommodation I was just pleased to have a roof over my head and the promise of a dry bed at the end of the day.

We bunked in together but were there only to sleep. The beauty of the mozzie dome was that it provided each of us with our own small piece of personal space. A sheet draped over the top of the mozzie dome made it even more private and homely. What was only slightly perplexing about our unusual accommodation was our access to the hospital, which required us to climb through a hole in a concrete wall. I never did get to find out why that hole existed — by chance or maybe someone had smashed it to connect our living area to the hospital compound.

My officer training buddy, Flying Officer Lara Gunn, had arrived two weeks earlier as part of an advance party and was enjoying much more salubrious living quarters inside the hospital compound, sharing a canvas tent with Army Nursing Officer, Captain Jo Harding. It was great to see her again and at this stage calls back home were restricted to one a week, so seeing Lara was like meeting up with family.

We were cautious not to implement any changes within the facility until after the departure of the Army team. Change is a necessary part of progression of any deployed facility but, as we would learn at the end of our own deployment, to watch that change undo months of your own work is difficult. The Army team appeared fatigued and we knew that they had endured greater hardship than we would come to know. Some staff had not left the hospital compound since their arrival the previous year because of the security dangers within Dili. Within a week of our arrival we farewelled our Army colleagues and then set to work.

The operating theatre was my 'place of parade', where I would report each day and at last get to carry out my main role of perioperative nurse. The daily routine included cleaning the operating theatre; attending to any sterilizing; ordering, unpacking and storing supplies; and, on occasion, undertaking a 'planned' theatre list. These lists included patients who were required to return to theatre for procedures such as the deliberate delayed closure of wounds, or removal of orthopaedic external fixation devices, which were commonly used to treat long bone fractures in the arms and legs. Otherwise, we were on standby for emergencies, and there was to be no shortage. We were routinely kept busy with surgical cases ranging from road trauma to acts of violence, such as stabbings and gunshot wounds, and the occasional appendicectomy. We were even called upon to assist one of the Army Dental Officers as she operated on a military working dog to replace a dental crown.

Most of our patients were local East Timorese. We also treated patients from the UN Forces, a small number of tourists and other visitors to the country. On occasions, the surgeons would receive permission to go beyond our mandate and provide non-emergency surgery to locals, procedures that so often turned out to be life-changing if not as dramatic as lifesaving. One such case included the removal of a 9-kilogram growth from the jawline of a local female. The growth had originated within a salivary gland and was so large she carried it in a sling fashioned from a sarong, in much the same way that the local women carried their babies. The inaccessibility to healthcare under Indonesian control and the fear of hospitals and what may happen to someone who was admitted was such that this woman was prepared to endure this condition rather than have it treated.

I found it difficult to understand why we were restricted to provide only eye, limb and lifesaving healthcare to the locals when we were working in a country in desperate need of medical care. Over time, I learned that the mandate under which we were working was to ensure that our very limited resources were used for those most in need, and that our larger responsibility was to support the sustainable redevelopment of the local health infrastructure. Dili had only one hospital, which would continue to be the main hospital facility in East Timor. It was being administered and staffed by the International Community of the Red Cross, who were also working towards its sustainable redevelopment. But the hospital we operated was temporary and had we acted as another permanent medical facility, our departure could create a devastating gap in healthcare to the local population. It was vital that we ensured that this did not occur.

As there was only one operating theatre team within our facility, we were on standby 24 hours a day, seven days a week. Some days flowed through the night and into the next, with the staff and the ever-operating instrument sterilizer pushed to their limits to provide the necessary care. As casualties arrived at the hospital gates, the resus siren would blare out loud enough that it could be heard throughout the compound and quite likely throughout the surrounding neighbourhood. Some days we treated a string of differing conditions: a fractured bone or acute appendicitis or a pregnant woman in obstructed labour. Other days, though, the casualties arrived en masse from one single incident — usually a motor vehicle crash.

Road rules in East Timor at the time were relaxed at best, and there seemed little requirement for drivers or passengers to observe any personal safety measures. The roof of a car, van or bus was just another place to find a seat. A family of mum, dad and two kids would ride on a motorbike and none of them would wear a safety helmet. Following the death of a young local man, the family arrived at the hospital to collect his body on the only mode of transport available to them, a motorbike. We quickly offered our support to transport the young man's body in a more appropriate way. On other days there were no surgical cases and we could give more time to maintaining the theatre complex and assist in the hospital inpatient ward, giving some respite to the ward nurses.

We felt safe at The Squeezer, our very own UNMILHOSP compound, but I began to feel something utterly new to me, and quite startling. I felt like I was suffocating, so much so I may just as well have entered a prison compound. From my perspective as a military nurse, I began to realize how the psychological stress or trauma of overseas deployment can come from more benign issues than I had expected. Of those people who have never been deployed, or who have done so but did not experience any personal hardship, some think that the adverse psychological impact of deployment exists only among those who have been in combat. There are even those who think that anyone else suffering such effects must be weak or, even worse, insincere and fraudulent. I don't believe that I suffered any adverse psychological effects from my first deployment to East Timor, but as a military nurse I was learning a valuable lesson about this condition.

The stress of deployment arises from an accumulation of things. You are separated from home and family and other social support networks, and there is a constant presence of others around you to the extent you never have a moment to yourself, whether working, eating, sleeping, showering, and toileting, exercising or relaxing. You can feel impotent trying to deal with issues back home. You must cope with restrictions placed on your diet, clothing, leisure activities and exercise options, along with the need to carry a weapon and the cultural differences between the host nation and coalition forces, which often mean curbing certain behaviours common to the Australian culture.

On this deployment, we were working alongside Egyptian army personnel who took great offence at Australian women exercising in shorts and T-shirts. We were living without air conditioning in temperatures in the mid thirties and with humidity above 90 per cent, but our Egyptian colleagues requested we show some modesty and cover more of our skin. I was starting to learn how confronting it can be for some of the youngest members of a deployed force to be thrown into a situation previously unknown to them. The accumulation of all the small sacrifices can add up to the greatest challenge they have ever faced.

As for my own feelings of suffocation, I was not going to let this new and unpleasant feeling get to me, especially since I was going to be confined here for six months. I was so determinedly eager to find ways to connect to the local community that I found it increasingly difficult to sit in a compound in someone else's country and know very little about its people. Fortunately for me the security situation in Dili improved, and it became possible to leave the compound and explore.

I jumped at the chance to accompany the Environmental Health Team whenever I could as they travelled around the city to conduct mosquito fogging of UN and Australian defence establishments. Competition was fierce for the vacant seat in the fogging vehicle as it provided a brief escape from the hospital compound and an insight into the devastation of Dili and its surrounding districts from where so many of our patients and their families came. I also leapt at the opportunity to take part in a hospital project at a local orphanage.

Two of the Air Force's most senior deployed airmen, Flight Sergeant Pete Mathey and Warrant Officer Michael Kearney, identified the Dalam Asrama orphanage, southeast of Dili in the Becora district, as being in need of support. A tiny group of four nuns provided care for about 50 children aged between five months and nineteen years. Not all of the children were orphans. Some had family in the more rural and isolated areas of East Timor and lived within the orphanage to be able to access education. Others came from families who simply could not afford to keep them. The nuns had received little support from any aid agencies and were doing their best to care for the children in three small houses infested with termites and generally in a very poor state of repair.

The tradesmen within our hospital group stepped up and in that wonderful, understated Australian way got on with the job as best they could — rewiring, painting and carpentry. That was followed up with a vegetable garden and food and toys were procured. When my workload allowed, I had the immense privilege of visiting the orphanage up to three times a week to provide English lessons to the nuns and the children. I was so very fortunate to have the support of my theatre team, fellow RN Flight Lieutenant Trish Mannix and theatre medics Flight Sergeant David Lee and Corporal Tim Netana, who would often remain at the hospital to provide theatre cover so that I could go out. On occasion, Tim would come along and bring his guitar to teach English through songs.

I did not have the first idea of how English could or should be taught but our audience seemed very happy with our efforts. I know we made a significant difference to their lives but it was our ability to leave the hospital compound and help make a positive difference in this struggling young nation that had such an enormous impact on our lives. I look back on my work at the Dalam Asrama orphanage as the highlight of my deployment to East Timor. It not only provided an escape from the hospital and my clinical role, it gave me a way to deliver aid to East Timor in my own way. I was working with the children of East Timor who did not need me for my skills but for a more personal type of care, and this was so fulfilling. These little people enriched my life, and my experiences with them would ultimately influence my future career decisions and alter the course of my life.

I also made an effort to get to know the locally employed civilians who worked alongside us within the hospital compound. In particular I spent time with 28-year-old Miss Irene and sixteen-year-old Miss Lilly, who were employed by the United Nations at UNMILHOSP as interpreters of Tetum (Timorese), Bahasa (Indonesian) and English. Both were available to the operating theatre team and assisted with translating as required. It struck me, that for my entire existence of 25 years Irene had been subjected to the rule of the invading Indonesian forces that had controlled her country. This was happening on the doorstep to my home and yet I was completely oblivious to it.

The Timorese had played a significant role in helping and protecting Australian soldiers fighting the Japanese in East Timor during the Second World War, and the East Timorese town of Balibo had been the site of the murder of five Australian-based journalists in 1975, the year of my birth. There were significant ties between our two countries and ongoing pressure from Australian media and veteran groups to assist in the plight of the East Timorese, who were suffering under Indonesian occupation. This had never featured in my education and was not discussed in my social circles while I was growing up. I have vague recollections of Free Timor protests at Salamanca Market in Hobart on Saturday mornings, or was that Free Tibet? Perhaps it was both.

To learn I had been an ignorant and sheltered citizen of the developed world came as a shameful slap in the face. It would still take many years of life and travel to realize that the citizens of countries or communities that I perceived to be disadvantaged did not require my charity, nor my pity, but rather my understanding. I would learn that in many ways their lives were so much richer than my own.

Irene and I became close friends spending much of our spare time together. She asked me to assist her with her English skills so that she would remain employable with the United Nations and she found great amusement teaching me Tetum. Most importantly, Irene taught me about East Timor and about her life prior to INTERFET. Through Lilly, the younger interpreter at UNMILHOSP, I also became acquainted with Miss Gabriela, a fifteen-year-old East Timorese girl also working as an interpreter for the United Nations. Gabriela and Lilly were school friends, although with the schools shut down following the violence, both were working hard to provide an income for their families. I was astounded that, despite the hardships these young girls had endured, they each spoke not three but four languages: Tetum, Bahasa, English and Portuguese, the official language of East Timor under the centuries long Portuguese rule and the language most spoken by older generations, such as the girls' grandparents.

My three newfound friends referred to me as Miss Sharon and I, in kind, referred to them as Miss Irene, Miss Lilly and Miss Gabriela. It was a common courtesy within East Timor to refer to those outside the immediate family with a title. The most often spoken English words among the East Timorese at that time were 'Mister' and 'Missus', and each was used to catch the attention of Australian service personnel. It was a local tradition that caught on among the Australian contingent of the hospital as we began to say each other's first name with the appropriate Miss or Mister, always respectful of rank of course.

It would also become a term of endearment in years to come, as a way of recognizing those with whom you had served in East Timor. Such simple gestures hold significance, indicating a deep connection between those who have shared this meaningful experience of life together; a connection which provides a deep sense of comfort that, in their company, certain things need no explanation. The wicked and amusing memories can be shared and laughed about, but the more difficult memories need not be mentioned. They are known and can rest comfortably in silence when those who experienced them are reunited.

The most obvious hardship among my new Timorese friends was the physical disability suffered by Miss Gabriela. As a child, she had scalded her left hand in a bath of hot water and with little access to appropriate and affordable healthcare her injury was not adequately treated. As a result, three of her fingers had contracted to fuse with her palm. As a UN employee in need of a simple surgical procedure to correct an injury she had long endured, Miss Gabriela was allowed a pro bono surgical procedure outside of the existing UN mandate. The Australian theatre team released her three fingers from her palm, allowing her to straighten them for the first time in her memory.

I saw more and more of Miss Gabriela as she returned for dressing changes and physiotherapy. She was an intelligent and ambitious young girl, but most memorably she was optimistic about the future of her country and the role she would assume in building it. I took a particular interest in her ventures, which would indeed pay huge dividends for herself and her country. To fulfill her ambition, she needed to return to her studies so Lara and I took it upon ourselves to help her with the fees required for her education. In Australia, the parents of a child might struggle to find the means by which to send him or her to a good school, where school fees might run into tens of thousands of dollars. This struggle by parents is universal, but in the case of Miss Gabriela, the cost was significantly less. It seemed that in order to secure her continued education, the fees would amount to the staggering cost of some cleaning supplies: namely mops, brooms, buckets and the like.

So Lara and I 'procured' the appropriate supplies and proudly delivered them to the school on Miss Gabriela's behalf, thus securing her contined education. Little did we know the immense flow-on effects of this incredibly simple act for her and her country. She would complete her schooling in East Timor and would then attend college and university in the United States. Lara and I would travel to the United States to witness her graduation from the Ivy League Cornell University in 2013 with a Masters of Public Administration. As promised, she took her knowledge and experience home to East Timor to assist in the continued progress of her country.

As my deployment continued, I was surprised to find that my Uncle Peter, a veteran of the Vietnam War, began to have some concerns about my tour of duty. Much to my astonishment, he somehow managed to get hold of the direct phone number for the inpatient ward of the UNMILHOSP and called to check up on me. This would have been no easy task. What's more, we had never been close as he had not lived in Tasmania during my lifetime and I simply knew of him as 'Uncle Peter on the mainland'. Now for some reason he was very concerned for my welfare, although he tried to hide it with inter-service rivalry humour. He claimed that I was unlikely to be in any danger as I was a 'Blue Orchid' — the banter used by members of the Army and Navy to refer to members of the Air Force, inferring that they are both precious and scarce. More seriously he wanted this Blue Orchid to be careful and look after myself. After all, he knew the dangers of military deployment and he had little remaining faith, if any, in the system that he felt had failed him and was now responsible for his big brother's little girl.

I became concerned that his knowledge of my deployment was causing him to reflect upon his own painful experiences. Uncle Peter was an early representative of the growing tide of men and women adversely affected by their service, with whom I would connect throughout my career as an Air Force Nursing Officer. At that point in my career, however, I thought his phone call no more than that of an over-concerned uncle and I told him he had nothing to be worried about.

I don't know how well I reassured him, but I felt safe. I knew that the security procedures we were required to follow were there to keep us protected from harm, so every day, no matter how secure I felt, I carried a rifle — when I ate, exercised, went to the toilet or shower and slept, it was with me. I felt more bothered about the dangers of mosquito-borne disease and the actions of the Egyptian males with whom we shared the compound, but I survived both. The greatest test of my resilience in this deployment, which neither Uncle Peter nor I could have seen, would soon unfold.

CHAPTER 3

FAR FROM HOME

2000 to 2003

As had become my habit, in the afternoons I would climb the stairs of the UNMILHOSP headquarters building, settling down somewhere towards the top. The white tiles, a feature of Indonesian architecture, provided a cool seat and the height of the staircase allowed me to capture the refreshing afternoon breeze. I took out my mobile phone and dialed home. What a 'war' this was becoming. One of the telephone services in Australia had begun to build a mobile phone network in East Timor whereas, just months before, my predecessors had had access to a satellite phone only. It was shared among dozens and rationed to 'ten minutes, per person, per day, perhaps'. I had finished my duties for the day and could now call Mum and Dad as if I were anywhere in Australia. It seemed too easy, too comfortable.

In years to come, some would argue that, although technology had all but removed the tyranny of distance between those deployed and their lives back home, it would also pose unforeseen challenges. Previous generations of servicemen and women would wait weeks or months for news from home. Now Thomas Gray's words would soon make so much sense: 'Where ignorance is bliss, 'tis folly to be wise.' It was a lesson I was to learn in the most tragic of circumstances that would leave me feeling devastated and powerless.

Mum was glad that I had called. She had something to tell me. She had found a lump in her left breast and it had been diagnosed as malignant. She was scheduled to undergo a lumpectomy in two days' time. I was speechless. I gazed at the changing colour of the Dili sky as the sun set behind me, taking with it the final day that I would ever feel the security of my mother's existence. My world was shifting uncontrollably.

My mother's surgery would include removing the lymph nodes in her left armpit that were closest to the affected breast, a procedure known to medicos as an axillary clearance. This was to be followed with a course of chemotherapy and radiotherapy. The medical approach was clinically clear, reasonable and logical for me, yet the recipient, the patient, the victim, was my mother. For most of my life there was hardly a moment without her presence, with never a thought there could be a moment without her. I had long acknowledged that by virtue of being deployed and not being with my family, my work and my mission were more important than my family. I had put my deployment first and my family not only respected that, but were also immensely proud of what I was doing. While talking on the phone, I had the most heart-wrenching urge to turn my back on this world to head back to Australia and comfort and care for my mother. Tears streamed down my cheeks as I pleaded with her, 'Mum, I want to come home!'

'It's okay, Sharon. There's nothing that you can do here. I didn't want to worry you. I will let you know how it goes as soon as I can.'

I was desperate to be with her and my colleagues saw this. This experience would become just one of the many times that the Air Force would demonstrate the concern and compassion it has for its people.

My Commanding Officer, Wing Commander Peter Clarke, immediately arranged compassionate leave for me that included return to Australia at service expense. I would be away for only a few days, but to my amazement my mother stymied my plans.

It was standard procedure for the Defence Community Organisation, which was responsible for arranging my return, to contact my mother to confirm that she needed me to return home. This was done to verify facts in support of the expenditure of Defence funds and analyse the effect my departure would have on the mission. However, my mother, overwhelmed by the contact from what she perceived as such a large and powerful organization as Defence, humbly and stoically reassured them that she was okay and that she understood the ADF's need to keep her daughter on operations was far greater than her need for the guidance and support that only a daughter with a health degree could offer at this time. My CO grumbled something about the efficiency of the organization in denying me leave but reassured me that I could take time out and return to Australia anyway. I would just need to fund the travel myself. It was the best that could be done but, as I was soon to discover, something else would stand in my way.

Despite earning the greatest pay packet of my life thus far, I discovered to my horror that my bank account was drained as quickly as I worked to fill it by my boyfriend back in Sydney. I had foolishly mistaken a joint bank account as a symbol of love and trust and I was too ashamed to admit my naivety to my parents. I could not tell them that their independent, and now apparently worldly successful daughter, was too weak to keep control of her own finances and was a victim of a condition known as 'sexually transmitted debt'. In order to support my new career my boyfriend had left a well-paid job that he loved in Hobart. He was having difficulty finding similar work in Sydney and he felt that, as I was the reason he was unemployed, I should support him until he did find work. I felt guilty for the sacrifices he had made so I just continued to enjoy my adventure and turned a blind eye to my lack of finances.

Neither the uniform of the ADF nor the skills and qualifications to serve humanity under the banner of the United Nations include lessons on how to control your bank account. Time and maturity would, but for now being almost destitute meant I would not be beside my mother in her greatest time of need, or in mine. Not wanting to reveal the truth of my circumstances, I thanked my CO for his offer and reassured him that my mother was being well cared for by my father and sisters and that there was no real reason for me to return home. But I was devastated. I did not blame anyone but myself. I made a meek threat to my partner that unless there was enough money in the bank upon my return to Australia to secure a home loan, then I would leave him and our relationship would be over.

I kept up the ruse of being in a happy and loving relationship and continued on with my work. My mother's surgery progressed to chemotherapy and radiotherapy and life at home began to change as my family attempted to adjust to having to care for her rather than having her care for them. I buried myself in my work, living a contradictory life where I was impotent to deal with the home front and my mother but I also got strength from being able to help make a difference in the lives of others in Timor. I continued to teach English to the orphans at the orphanage, to work hard in my clinical role as a nurse and to build my friendships with the locally employed civilians and their families. Amid all this, two clinical cases I was involved with would generate more interest from others outside my deployment than anything else that I had achieved or endured.

In a sleepy haze, after having worked all night, I heard a beseeching plea, 'Ma'am you have to get up,' as the mosquito net that surrounded my bed was shaken. My mind conducted a quick scan and reminded me that, yes, I was still in Timor, I was sleeping in the mid morning after having worked all night and did not have to get up, and I was so tired.

'No! I've worked all night. I don't have to be up right now.'

'But, Ma'am, you don't understand. There's a fractured penis in the operating theatre!'

Now I was awake. A fractured penis! This was not supposed to happen to me again. Back in Hobart, on one of the very rare occasions I worked a weekend shift in the operating theatre, we were just concluding the morning's operating list when the theatre suite doorbell rang. I was sent out to see who was there. Opening the door, I was greeted by a senior urologist who enquired about the availability of the theatre and staff. Being the most junior member of the team I was not foolish enough to think that I knew the answers to his questions, and I said as much. This, of course, frustrated a man of such importance.

'Well, Sister,' — nurses were called Sister back in 'his day' — 'I suggest that you find out. I have a fractured penis and I need an operating theatre.'

I wasn't convinced I had heard him correctly, but I certainly wasn't about to question him either. After a very quick glance at his groin, I pondered the chances that this was some perverted joke at the expense of a junior theatre nurse. The expression on his face certainly didn't support my theory, so I politely excused myself to check on the availability of the operating theatre for one poor gentleman, who had an apparent proclivity for a little rough play in the boudoir, and who indeed had a genuine injury. What I certainly remember of this most bizarre clinical day, was the statement made by the treating urologist: 'You're very fortunate, Sister. This is a very rare injury that most clinicians will never ever see in their career. You certainly won't see this again.' His idea of such good fortune was different to mine.

Now, in East Timor, awake but tired and bleary eyed, my career quota of one fractured penis was to be surpassed. I dragged myself out of bed, still not convinced that the injury existed, but duty bound to at least report to the theatre. The Australian general surgeon was assessing the patient and he requested the theatre be readied for a fractured penis repair. The foreign serviceman to be operated on explained that he had fallen out of bed that morning, landing upon his erect penis.

Only a few short weeks later, yet another foreign serviceman from the same region of the country was brought to our operating theatre with the identical condition. No, it's not something that is contagious, although even I had begun to wonder about this. This second injury was reported as being sustained when the man rolled over in bed onto his erect penis. There may have been some rather hard beds in that part of the world, but this explanation was even less plausible than the first, and then reports filtered through, referring to acts of bestiality, which sadly seemed more likely.

There would be many notable events during my Air Force career, yet it has never ceased to amaze me that those incidents would be so defining. Years later, when I spoke to Australian healthcare workers about my time in Timor, they would often enquire if I knew the story of the fractured penises. I couldn't help but begin to think that perhaps I was the story: the nurse who beat all the odds and succeeded in witnessing three fractured penises in one career! What a gal. For those more curious, a penile fracture is in fact more of a rupture, as there are no bones in the penis. The rupture occurs when a penis is erect and is subjected to a sudden force that increases the pressure inside the penile tissues, so much so that they tear. It's a bit like bursting a balloon and is said to be very painful.

I grew up quickly during my first deployment to East Timor. I arrived just on 25 years of age and was there for six and a half intense months. I had begun this journey with the idealistic and patronizing notion that I had the skills to save the world, one 'disadvantaged' person at a time. I ended it with the harsh realization that, despite living in a country of abundance and privilege, I lacked the courage to protect myself from financial disadvantage and was equally incapable of providing care to my own family in their time of need. The most empowering thing to come from this period of my service was the loss of my innocent belief in the great Australian fairytale that little girls grow up to become wives, mothers and 'joint' homeowners, and would live happily ever after.

When I returned to Australia in August 2000, I finally had the opportunity to go home and care for Mum as I had originally wanted to. She had undergone her treatment in Hobart and there was no evidence of any secondary tumours. At the conclusion of her chemotherapy and radiotherapy she was given an all clear, but with a caution to be vigilant with her health. No recurrence of tumours within five years would provide the greatest indicator that the cancer had been completely removed. We spent countless hours together discussing my time and my work in East Timor. I knew that one side of her had hoped that I would live up to my side of our perfect plan for me to now return home for good but, unlike anyone else in my life, she also understood the passion I had developed for nursing within the Air Force. She reassured me that she was okay and encouraged me to follow my dreams.

By Christmas 2002, secondary tumours would appear in her liver and her bones and Mum would recommence chemotherapy, this time with a vague hope of a cure, but most significantly in a desperate fight for time with her family. On top of my feeling of deep sadness that I had not been with my mother during her early diagnosis, I was to learn that my partner had called my financial bluff — there was no money in our account when I arrived home.

To be young and foolish is not uncommon but it would be another two years before I finally tired of working so hard to be broke. I had felt so guilty that he had left his home and family to follow my career but I had also, naively and immaturely, believed I was in love. Perhaps I had also underestimated the emasculation he may have felt when I asked him to reject the traditional Australian gender roles and follow my career in preference to his own. Regardless of the reasons our relationship ended bitterly and I was left to continue in my service alone.

As my personal life crumbled, my professional life advanced. I was appointed to take charge of the Operating Theatre Complex back in Australia at the base where I was first posted, 3 Hospital at Richmond on the edge of Sydney. The operating theatre comprised a theatre, a procedure room mostly used for endoscopy, a two-bed recovery room and a central sterilizing store. It was similar to what might be found in most rural hospitals across Australia. We operated five days a week and employed civilian surgeons and anaesthetists, some of whom served in the Defence Reserves. The surgery included specialties of general, orthopaedic, dental, ear, nose and throat. Patients requiring critical care were treated at larger civilian facilities.

This role let me use the specialist nursing skills that I loved and it also allowed me to begin to explore and refine my leadership skills. My time in East Timor had further clarified my role as a Nursing Officer and a perioperative nurse within the Air Force, and now I was keen to develop these skills further. I was to learn a great deal from the outstanding team at the Richmond base but faced another hurdle. Soon after I took up the role of Officer-in-Charge (OIC), my appointment was challenged. A senior Air Force Medical Officer, who was not a part of 3 Hospital, raised concerns about my apparent lack of a tertiary qualification within perioperative nursing. It had not previously been an issue as far as the position was concerned and I was more than ably supported by two very experienced civilian perioperative Registered Nurses.

My senior Nursing Officer, Squadron Leader Jennifer Roe, defended my competence and suitability based upon a thorough record of my civilian experience and my operational experience in East Timor. Even so, I recognized the concerns that had been raised as valid and a progressive step for Air Force Nursing, and so I went on to gain my Postgraduate Diploma of Perioperative Nursing. I had to really apply myself outside of my normal working hours, but received enormous support from my senior civilian Registered Nurse, Helen Ross. The other great achievement at this time was on my three-year anniversary in the Air Force when I received my first promotion. I was now a Flight Lieutenant.

My new role within the operating theatre was in fact two appointments in one. As well as being in charge of the operating theatre I was commanding a highly specialized unit that sounded so dramatically exciting but which was more often than not a source of disappointment. I was in charge of the Fly Away Surgical Team or FAST, and that was its aim. The FAST was a lightweight, air transportable and rapidly deployable operating theatre. It was designed to be put into the cargo compartment of an Air Force transport aircraft and be carried anywhere in the world a field operating theatre was needed, and then be rapidly set-up, ready to provide life-saving surgery — sort of like a mini *M*A*S*H*.

The FAST, despite its incredible capability, rarely needed to be deployed. I, like many theatre OICs before me, seemed to become tied to this operational asset. We would go through the excitement of loading it onto Air Force aircraft, unloading it at a forward location close to where a potential need was and then waiting, ready to move into an area to set it up and start operating, only to pack it up and take it home again. My connection with the FAST began to prevent me from being deployed. If it didn't go, I didn't go. This came home to me forcefully during the Bali bombings on 12 October 2002.

I was required to remain at RAAF Base Richmond on standby with the FAST should it need to be transported to Bali. The FAST could have been well used if quickly deployed but by the time that became apparent, it was no longer needed. The injured were stabilized and repatriated by Air Force aircraft for medical attention back in Australia. My deployment to East Timor had convinced me of my love of operational nursing, and despite my love of perioperative nursing and my appointment as OIC Theatre at 3 Hospital, it was clear that if I wanted to deploy again, I needed to separate myself from 3 Hospital and the FAST. It became imperative for me to move on.

In the two years after my time in Timor, I had walked away from a painful relationship and in the process I had lost my home and almost everything I owned, forcing me to return to live on the base in the Officers' Mess accommodation. I had also become tied to a deployable asset that seemed would never be deployed, and neither would I. Unhappy, I decided to surrender my appointment and left my dedicated and loyal team to head north to Queensland to accept a posting to RAAF Base Amberley, west of Brisbane.

After my departure from Richmond there was a period of wide-ranging restructure within the ADF, with the usual jargon of strategic reform and rationalization. In the Air Force and across the ADF this resulted in medical theatres being increasingly civilianized and then closed. In saving dollars, we lost a construct that provided valuable mentorship of junior ADF healthcare workers by more senior and experienced workers whose greatest value resided in the fact that they were veterans of service. We lost the ability to care for our own in Australia, as we would be required to do so overseas. The connection between the fighting force and those who would care for them in battle was beginning to change.

It was not until much later, when strategic alliances developed between Defence health and state health institutions, that such valuable collaboration and mentorship would be re-established and done so on a much greater scale than could have occurred in the confines of ADF health centres. In some large teaching hospitals, such as the Royal Brisbane Women's Hospital, Defence Reserve Medical Officers can now work in their civilian role to mentor junior Air Force Medical Officers. The greatest failing to date, however, is that it appears to only exist within the Medical Officer category and does not extend to other healthcare roles. But I am confident that this is a problem that will be resolved with time and experience.

My move from Richmond to Amberley provided me with a fresh

start. In 2003 I settled into life in the Officers' Mess more readily than I had in Richmond. I was able to explain that I had been posted here and I was looking to buy a home in the region and until then I would be living in the Mess. Back in Richmond it had been too painful to reveal why I was living in the Mess.

I enjoyed the climate and smaller city lifestyle of nearby Brisbane, a sub-tropical contrast to my upbringing in cool Tasmania. I became firm friends with fellow Mess resident Flight Lieutenant Doug Rawlinson, who originally came from the Gold Coast, about an hour's drive away, and he was able to help me orientate to a new state and city. We were easily the oldest officers residing in the Mess, living alongside the much younger pilots who flew Caribou transport aircraft and the navigators on the F-111 bombers.

We both enjoyed the social aspect of Mess life yet eagerly spent most weekends exploring the local housing market together, as we each aspired to buy homes off-base. As we ventured into new romantic relationships, me with Conway, an Army helicopter pilot from Townsville, and Doug with Cate, a child psychologist from Brisbane, the Mess lifestyle became increasingly cramped and uncomfortable. I was finally able to buy my first home in October, in Ipswich, not far from the base, and Doug would soon follow suit, proposing to marry the beautiful Cate.

During the initial six weeks of my posting to Amberley, I worked for a senior Reserve Nursing Officer, Wing Commander Jenny Lumsden, within the Reserve Health Cell of the headquarters of the newly formed Health Services Wing (HSW). HSW commands all Air Force Health units, providing expeditionary health support, aeromedical evacuation, aerospace medicine and garrison health support within Australia and overseas. The Air Force Reserve was our 'part time' force and, for Air Force Health, was indispensable. The jobs may have been part time for the Air Force but their full-time jobs were in civilian healthcare. They brought with them the latest updates in medical practice and care from that sector. After this brief period of duty, I took up my official posting at the nearby No. 1 Air Transportable Health Squadron, which was air transportable in name and readiness but its actual day-to-day role was to provide health support to RAAF Base Amberley. Operationally it sent smaller teams from within the squadron to locations all over the world to provide health support to the Defence operations overseas.

I had been a big fish in a big pond as an OIC within 3 Hospital and was now a very little fish in an even bigger headquarters environment. I was comfortable engaging with the Reserve members of the HSW, some of whom I had already served alongside in both Richmond and East Timor. The Officer Commanding HSW at that time was the inaugural commander, Medical Officer, Group Captain Amanda Dines. The CO of the headquarters was an Air Force Nursing Officer, Wing Commander Michael Paterson. I enjoyed working for these senior officers so much in those short six weeks that I offered to exchange my posting to remain at HSW. That was deemed to be unnecessary, as another Nursing Officer was already due to arrive in the position. So I moved to 1 Air Transportable Health Squadron as originally planned.

Within this new team I was still a small fish in a small pond. There was no operating theatre, so my specialist skills were of little significance in the day-to-day operation of the health centre. So I began to learn the roles and responsibilities of the outpatient Nursing Officer. It was not an area that really interested me, but I understood and accepted its importance in my nursing role within the Air Force. Before too long I was rewarded with the opportunity to once again deploy to East Timor. As I had already been there I was offered a split six-month rotation in 2004 with fellow Nursing Officer, Flight Lieutenant Belinda Ball, meaning that each of us would deploy for only three months and Belinda took the first rotation.

CHAPTER 4

RETURN TO EAST TIMOR

2004

The rush of getting ready to deploy subsided as, along with other ADF members, I sat and waited at Darwin airport for the flight to Dili. The policies and procedures of the ADF ensured that I was at least logistically ready to undertake my overseas duty. Paperwork and database checking at my home base of Amberley, along with a week of pre-deployment training at Randwick Army Barracks in Sydney, had me ready to go. I was physically, medically and dentally fit. I was proficient in handling and firing the F88 rifle and Browning 9mm pistol. My CO had released me for duty and I was deemed psychologically fit and willing to deploy. I had volunteered for this deployment and I had no hesitation in heading back for another tour in East Timor. This time, though, I was to be an Aeromedical Evacuation (AME) nurse on an emergency medical service helicopter.

Mum by this time was still undergoing treatment for metastatic breast cancer but was still feeling well. We had discussed my ability to return home if needed. She was excited for me and encouraged me to go, but I was still not convinced about leaving her. I had returned home to Tassie to see her before I left, and to check with her oncologist to make sure that I really wasn't needed. Everyone seemed happy for me to just get on with my life. Mum wanted to spend as much time with Dad as she could while continuing to be a part of the lives of her children and grandchildren. I was torn between wanting her to need me just a little bit more and excited to be doing the job that I loved. I said goodbye to my family and headed to Randwick Barracks in Sydney, where I would also visit and farewell my closest friends.

I had been fortunate to share the major milestones of my military career with my dearest friend Lara, and this one would be no exception. During our time at Officer Training School Lara had impressed the drill sergeant with her drive and determination. She was appointed parade commander for our graduation parade, proving her physical form did not disguise her command presence. We wondered however if her petiteness might not cause the scabbard of her ceremonial sword to leave marks on the parade ground. All joking aside, later in her career I would watch on with pride as she was honoured for her exemplary contribution to Air Force Health, including her graduation in the top 3 per cent of the Australian Command and Staff course — the ADF's course preparing senior officers for command — and her appointment as the first Air Force Pharmacy Officer to command a Health Squadron.

Lara and I had lived side-by-side during our training at Point Cook in 1999, were deployed together in 2000 to East Timor, and worked together at 3 Hospital for the ensuing two years before my posting to Amberley and hers to Randwick. As I made final preparations to depart, she hugged me goodbye and told me how she wished I didn't have to go. She had enjoyed having me around for the week, and I had enjoyed her company amidst my final preparations to leave Australia. The day before, I had said farewell to Conway, my boyfriend of less than five months.

As a full-time member of the Army, flying Chinook helicopters for the 5th Aviation Regiment based in Townsville in Queensland's far north, he was required back at base. As a woman, I felt he should have put his life on hold for one more day to say goodbye to me. But as an Air Force Officer, I accepted that he was the busiest man I knew, and appreciated so much the leave he had somehow managed to secure to visit me in Sydney. He had travelled the world often and had already been deployed to Timor twice within his career and he couldn't understand what attraction there was for me to volunteer to return. We certainly differed. He was ambitious and practical in achieving his goals; I was idealistic and wanting to save the world for those that inhabited it, no matter where on earth they had begun their lives. Separation from friends and family was the only misgiving I ever felt about my role as a nurse in the Air Force, otherwise I loved the excitement and unpredictable nature of my life. Now I was off on my next adventure.

We had travelled to Darwin on a commercial flight to make what would be for me an unusual connection to Timor. On arrival at Darwin, I walked out onto the airfield and boarded the SAAB Metro commuter plane, nicknamed the 'pencil plane' because it was very long and slim and seated only twelve passengers in two rows of single seats. I felt a little apprehensive as I realized that the last person to board the flight was the pilot, and that he was responsible for closing the door behind us. There was no cabin crew. The crouching pilot pointed out the Esky ice cooler strapped in up the front as our source of 'self-serve' drinks and snacks. Although I am certain there was a safety brief, no well-groomed flight attendant with a calming, helpful smile delivered it.

'Here we go,' I thought. 'Just my next adventure in life. Wait 'til I email home about the trip in the pencil plane!'

As I relaxed into the soothing hum of the engines and the buoyancy of flight, my thoughts turned to my family and friends. I considered the legal processes I had navigated during recent weeks to ensure that they would be protected in the event that I did not return from this trip. As part of standard preparation for deployment I had revised my Last Will and Testament and appointed Powers of Attorney. I smiled at the thought of the older Air Force Legal Officer that processed my affairs, bemused by the fact that a single 29-year-old woman owned property and yet did not have a husband to leave it to. My Last Will and Testament would have been straightforward if only I had followed the social conventions of his generation. How dare I complicate the legal process with family, friends and a boyfriend, all worthy of a slice of my estate? An unnerving thought broke through my humorous musing. If I never returned to Australia, if I were to lose my life in East Timor, it would actually be okay — everything had been taken care of. The ADF had adequately prepared me to not return. I rested my head against the tiny window of the aircraft, my thoughts lost in the peacefulness of the downy, white clouds, and surprisingly I felt an immense sense of calm.

As we crossed the south coast of the island of Timor, I searched the landscape below for familiar landmarks, attempting to get my bearings and reacquaint myself with this foreign shore. Deployments to Timor had become so commonplace for Air Force Nursing Officers that almost all of us had been at least once and the competition to get there had decreased — it was now possible to volunteer rather than be directed to return. The civilian nurses I had trained with back in Tassie were always interested to hear of the adventurous nature of my less conventional nursing career. I had to admit that my Air Force nursing career had not yet been long enough for me to not share their naive excitement at the thrill of visiting such foreign and exciting places where I could put my skills to work. The green, jungle-clad mountains reached up below me, with brief glimpses of tiny villages to show human life. The island was very small but the vast lack of any infrastructure made it seem much larger. I would fly in and out of this amazing region over the coming months to assist in delivering aid, in a job far from the creature comforts

In December 1995 I graduated from the University of Tasmania with a Bachelor of Nursing. It was a proud day for me, but even more so for my parents. [Author]

Every new recruit has a photo of themselves in their uniform, some more embarrassing than others. [Author]

Officer Training helps to develop teamwork and problem-solving skills; although, I am not sure which of life's problems would require me to help pass a person through some crochet. [Author]

The East Timorese children would often stop at the front gate of the hospital to say hello. [Author]

The view of the UN Military Hospital from 'The Squeezer'. The red-roofed building is the main entrance to the compound with the operating theatre out of view to the right and the line of tents on the left being the outpatients tents. [Author]

The salubrious sleeping quarters for my early days in East Timor. The mozzie domes provided little privacy or soundproofing, but kept the mosquitoes and attendant malaria at bay. Very little airflow existed in the room and none in the mozzie domes. The heat and humidity made any rest almost impossible. [Author]

The inspiring Miss Gabriela on her graduation day from Cornell University. [Author]

The aircraft, Callsign UN079, that changed my life. [Author]

ANZAC Day 2004. I am fit and healthy and enjoying my role as an operational Air Force Nursing Officer. *Left to right*: Corporal Maria Brown, me, Flying Officer Sharon Higgins. [Author]

UN079 in its final resting position. It was a testament to the skill of the pilots that the cabin structure remained relatively intact despite the impact of the crash. [Source unknown]

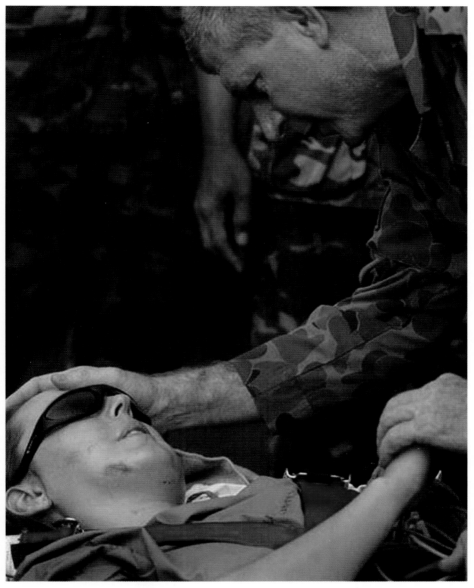

Lieutenant Colonel Bradford, having placed his sunglasses on me to shield my eyes from the sun, says goodbye as I am about to be loaded onto the Medevac jet. [ADF Media Archive]

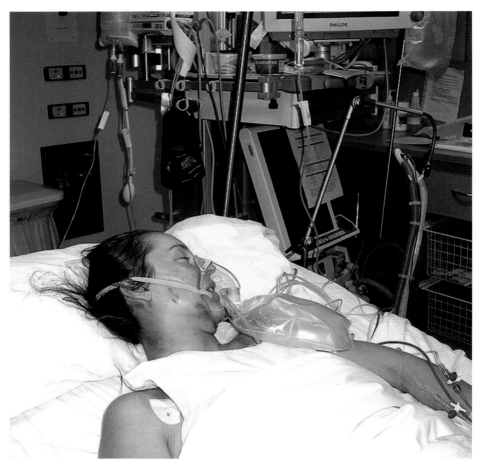

Above Swollen and not looking too crash hot … no pun intended. My jaw had been operated on but the complications during the operation resulted in a brief period where I stopped breathing and required resuscitation. I don't remember seeing a bright light, though! [Author]

Right Learning to walk again was certainly a challenge. I was wearing the back brace under my new pyjamas that were provided by Conway. He was quite chuffed that so many of the nurses there complimented him on his taste. I would have thought he would have been chuffed at seeing me walk again … but fashion trumps all, I guess. [Author]

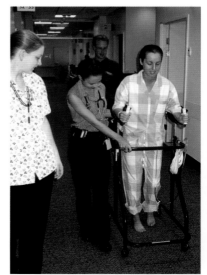

and resources to which I had become so accustomed, but all that just added to the excitement.

Dili airport had changed since my last visit. It was much more developed than in 2000, so much so I could have been arriving at the homely and cozy airport in Hobart. But as I stepped out of the aircraft I was greeted by the all too familiar wall of heat and humidity and that distinct tropical smell — my olfactory memory alone instantly reassured me I was back in Dili. In 2000, I had dragged my bags and personal belongings from the hull of a C-130 Hercules transport aircraft and climbed into the back of a military truck for my journey to The Squeezer, our beloved UNMILHOSP. Now I walked through the airport terminal with my carry-on bag and waited to collect my luggage from a carousel. And transport to my living quarters would now be in a much more comfortable UN Land Rover.

At the baggage carousel I met my welcoming party — members of the Air Force AME team of which I was about to become a member. It was comforting to be welcomed by familiar friends and colleagues and to sense their excitement in seeing me. The AME team consisted of two Medical Officers, two Nursing Officers, and a Medical Assistant. Three of them were from my own unit at Amberley and had arrived in Timor three months earlier when the deployment began. My arrival meant their out-of-country leave roster could now start. The disadvantage for me of arriving halfway through the team's deployment was not only that I would have to transition into an already established team but, in the coming days, the team would be divided and reformed many times to allow for those completing the six-month tour to have their much-needed leave. It was to be an unsettled period for all of us.

The selection, formation and deployment of small teams often present unique challenges. It requires preparing a group of people, sometimes strangers, to live and work together for lengthy periods in close and often stressful circumstances. Getting the right people for such a mission is crucial. But even under the best circumstances there will be people desperate to escape the team and start their leave. This deployment had been so stressful for some that they would choose not to return. During my 2000 deployment I formed strong and lasting bonds with team members and the locals, but I was realistic enough to know that the country and its people who had so captivated me before would have changed, even if I wasn't fully aware what those changes were.

In Dili now there were fewer restrictions upon the movement of ADF personnel around the city. It was not uncommon to eat out at local restaurants, and it was not unusual to drop by a local café for a coffee or freshly squeezed fruit juice. Dili had become a thriving small metropolis, benefiting from the incomes of the UN personnel residing in the city. Entrepreneurial Australians, mostly from the Northern Territory, were opening a range of hospitality and tourism businesses. My living accommodation had improved drastically. I shared an air-conditioned demountable hut divided into two separate living quarters with a female Army officer. We each had a single bed, a wardrobe, power outlet and an electric light. Such comfort contrasted with life under the mozzie dome of my last deployment. We even had access to a swimming pool, as the Australian civilian aircrew contracted to the United Nations to fly the EMS helicopter lived in a hotel on the Dili Esplanade, which had a restaurant and a pool. Similar to my time in 2000, the AME team was on call 24/7, but this time were able to roster staff so that at least one member of the team could relax each day. I could almost enjoy a day off.

I felt somewhat guilty to be enjoying such luxuries when it was evident that the conditions the local population continued to live with had not risen to anywhere near the sort of comfort we were enjoying. The UN mandate under which we worked remained similar to that of 2000: providing healthcare for those personnel assigned to the UN mission and to provide eye, limb and lifesaving healthcare for East Timorese locals. As was the case back then, the bulk of our AME workload was in support of the local population, another sign that access to healthcare in East Timor remained parlous and denied to most of the population.

The most shocking and appalling example of this came with the release of autopsy details of a twelve-year-old East Timorese girl who died in the year before our arrival. She had choked to death on intestinal worms. She had asphyxiated when hundreds of worms crawled from her stomach into her oesophagus and mouth seeking food and, in doing so, had blocked her trachea. The girl could have been 'wormed' for less than a dollar but instead lay lifeless on a cold slab in the Coroner's Office, killed by a parasite that most Australian dogs and cats are protected from.

The feel of this mission was very different. The hero-cum-celebrity status of ADF personnel that I experienced in 2000 had been replaced by a deep-seated resentment toward Australia over the oil resources battle in the Timor Gap — the line between Timor and Australia at the edge of the continental shelf and the site of deposits of hydrocarbons ready for human exploitation. Now that East Timor was an independent country, it laid economic claim to the undersea resources up to the median line between the two countries. This meant the political climate between our countries had changed from one of salvation to that of diplomatic dispute. Still, this was a positive indicator that East Timor was embracing its hard-fought independence and survival as the world's newest nation.

The disparity of wealth between the Timorese and their UN saviours sadly translated into a greater safety threat to UN personnel and an interaction with the local community that was not as good as it had been in my earlier mission. We could experience greater freedom to enjoy social activities but we had to be much more wary of how, where and with whom we travelled. We were required to wear a sidearm or carry a rifle in what the ADF calls 'force protection measures'. One outcome of all this was that the Dalam Asrama orphanage, which I had supported in 2000, was in a little backstreet on the outskirts of Dili and was considered too dangerous for me to visit. I could not go back and visit the children and the nuns. I felt so close to them and yet so far away.

A friend from 2000 that I could visit was Miss Gabriela, now known to me as Gabi. I had been Mana Sharon to her, *mana* being the Tetum word for 'older sister'. I still had the title, and it was one of such immense respect that each time I read it or heard it from Gabi my heart would swell with pride just a little. I have a younger sister, Tina, whom I adore, and to be blessed with another has been my incredible good fortune. The challenges of my role within the AME team were in such contrast to the fulfillment I enjoyed in helping Gabi to make the most of her future. She was an intelligent and dedicated young woman who would never be constrained by her past or that of her nation. She represented the possibility of a bright future for her new country.

I loved my job as an Air Force Nursing Officer but, as with my first deployment, I continued to reassess whether it still satisfied my first aims, which were to use my nursing skills to deliver aid to those most in need, particularly if it kept me so far from Mum. I felt that this deployment still met my needs, but resolved to defer any uncertain feelings I had until I took leave and returned to Australia. This would allow me to consider my next step, free of the removed-from-reality nature of operational deployment. I had only ten days to go before the end of my three-month deployment when something so drastic happened that it changed everything. It began with an afternoon nap.

CHAPTER 5

'MAYDAY!'
'MAYDAY!'

June 2004

My stomach was full, my head was beginning to ache in the midday heat and there was no reason for the team to return to the Aeromedical Staging Facility, our primary place of work as an AME team. It was the perfect recipe for what I referred to as a nanna nap, what others might know as a mini siesta, a kip. Whoever said war was 95 per cent boredom and 5 per cent terror had possibly spent some time in Dili. For us, the terror was more likely to be adrenalin-fuelled excitement and alacrity as we were called to our duties as an AME team. We were the insurance policy of the UN operation, the 'just in case' clause. As much as we thrived on being able to assist those in their dire time of need, our busyness ultimately meant someone else's misfortune.

I was on call that fateful day and needed to be responsive. As I settled on my bed, I knew there would be no rest while my flying boots were still on. I convinced myself that in an emergency I could pull them on and tighten them without delay, and so I sat them neatly at the end of my bed, poised and ready for action. I lay back on the bed and dialled

Conway's number. A lull in the day and the desire to relax was the perfect excuse to hear his voice. We chatted. He was amused by my nanna-nap plans, wished me a good sleep and promised to talk to me later in the evening. With thoughts of home and the comfort of Conway's conversation, I drifted off into my afternoon slumber.

The shrill of the AME phone wrenched me from my dreams. The voice penetrating the haze of my peaceful sleep uttered just the right combination of words to rouse an adrenalin rush capable of setting those action-ready flying boots into flight. Without a second thought they were on my feet. I raced to the vehicle to meet the doctor and head off to the heliport, an old airfield away from the main Dili airport where the helicopters were based alongside our Aeromedical Staging Facility.

A local East Timorese woman in the mountain village of Same (pronounced Sah-may), about 90 kilometres south of Dili as the crow flies, was in obstructed labour and had been so for such an extended period that her unborn baby was likely to have already died and her own life was now in danger. Our team met the civilian aircrew at the helicopter to prepare for the mission. After nearly five-and-a-half years of Air Force Health teams performing this task we had become quite skilled, and about to demonstrate our raison d'être once again. As I loaded the last of the AME kit into the helicopter I heard the familiar and friendly voice of the pilot: 'Okay, who's up front today?' Confused, I turned to look at him. There were only two seats up front and two pilots. What was he talking about? His smile answered my question.

'I'm up front,' I answered cheekily. 'I'm tired of riding in the back, and I think it's about time I got to ride in the front.' He laughed at me. At the controls of the Bell 212 and in the briefing room, the aircrew were very serious and always professional. I grinned, checked that my pistol was secure in its holster, having just completed my drills to ensure it was unloaded, grabbed my helmet and jumped into my rightful seat, the one in the back. I sat on the second seat from the left, leaving the seat by the door empty.

I loved to fly, particularly the low-altitude flight of a helicopter, and I always sat as close to the doors as I could to enjoy the view. Why I didn't sit next to the door on that particular day I do not know. But I would learn that this simple change in action might have saved my life. I had strapped the AME 'Thomas' Pack, a heavy backpack containing medical supplies, into the seat to the right of me. The AME doctor, Squadron Leader David Leaf, occupied the seat to the right of that. He had arrived in East Timor at the same time as me but only to cover the team's period of leave. He had been asked to stay on for the entire mission to cover a staffing shortage and today would be our first AME together.

Seated to his right was the rescue crewman, Greg. I plugged my flying helmet's headset into the intercom system, grateful that in this particular aircraft I would be 'on comms' for the entire flight and able to communicate with all members of the crew. The other helicopter available to us had one less intercom cable than the helicopter in which we were flying, UN079. It was always the AME nurse who was deemed the least important in communicating with the rest of the team on those flights. However, hand signals and written notes did manage the job, even if more onerously. Today's flight would be so much simpler.

The mood aboard was friendly and jovial as we lifted off into the sky above Dili and my thoughts quickly returned to the patient we had been called in to evacuate. It was 1510 hours on 2 June 2004. We headed south towards Same, which was on the other side of the steep mountain range that formed the backbone of the long but narrow island, its peaks rising to 3000 metres in places. The pregnant woman for whom we were en route was receiving medical assistance at the Same Clinic from the local doctors. I listened as the aircrew discussed how they would make their approach to the village and noted that the weather around the mountain range may prolong our flight or even prevent our access as the mountain range, and the gaps through which aircraft could fly, appeared to be obscured by low cloud and rain. Soon, vision reduced significantly and it was difficult to see the ground.

It began to rain and rivulets of water danced on the Perspex windows of the helicopter, smashed by the rotor wash and slipstream. I knew that the pilots were having a hard time transiting the mountains as I listened to them coming up with plans to find a gap through which to navigate. We attempted two separate crossings but each was thwarted by the rapidly deteriorating weather. The pilots decided to try a third route and even discussed a fourth contingency. I remember seeing the windscreen wipers flicking across the canopy glass and wondering how the pilots could see. I peered through the window of the cargo door and saw nothing but rain and cloud, which would make the village very difficult to locate.

We finally crossed the mountains and headed towards the village, which lay in the piedmont — from the Italian word meaning 'foot of the mountain'. We made two approaches to try to find the village. The third attempt revealed a break in the low cloud and we could see the ground and the outline of a small riverbed. I could hear that the aircrew were familiar with this riverbed and they agreed to attempt to follow it. I had not been to Same before and was not familiar with the landmarks being discussed. The helicopter was manoeuvered through two downward spiralling descents. I could now see the ground and it remained visible to me through the side doors. The rain got heavier, severely hampering visibility through the front windscreen. I again watched the windscreen wipers working feverishly. Even now, so many years later, the sound of heavy rain drags me back to this moment.

The rescue crewman had opened the right-hand door to get better visibility of the ground. The rain was streaming through the open door. I was not concerned for my own safety, as I was aware that the crew was working very hard and I thought that we simply might not reach Same that day. My concern was for the patient whose life may be depending upon our arrival. The pilots attempted a third spiralling but wider descent. Looking back this seemed to be when we may have passed the point of no return. On the intercom, a male voice yelled, 'We're going in! Brace, brace, brace!'

We're what? Brace means to 'assume the crash position'! I had trained to respond to such words, but hearing them I felt the briefest moment of disbelief. Through the front windscreen I could now see that we were racing toward the trees. There was something very wrong: we were in dire trouble. Suddenly visibility appeared clear, which meant we were really close to the trees and flying towards the ground. I followed my training. I leaned forward, crossed my arms across the front of my shins and grabbed my ankles. I looked to my right to observe the doctor assuming the same position. As his actions mirrored my own it assured me that this was really happening. He would later tell me he did not brace forward but sat upright. Had I seen what I wanted to?

'Mayday, mayday . . .'

This was it! So sudden. So surreal. So powerless to alter the rapid change of course my life was about to take. The aircrew speedily followed their drills as we in the back sat motionless. Waiting. Helpless. I gripped my ankles harder and held myself firm as the world rushed past me. I was overwhelmed by fear as I accepted that I was about to die, and if I didn't die, I was certainly about to break.

My life didn't flash before my eyes, but in an instant I thought of my loved ones and I knew that they would all survive this, only Conway would be left alone. Despite the fear, I felt a calming peace and a deep sorrow for Conway. He was the last person in my life that I had spoken to and he was the one who would be left to deal with this alone. It was a feeling for which there was no peace. I knew that in a profoundly cruel way I was about to hurt the people I loved the most and there was nothing I could do to stop it from happening. My final memory of this moment was of the most intense fear intermingled with the most intense sorrow. Silently I apologized to the man I loved and the light of the world turned black.

'Come on, darling, we have to get out.' I recognized the voice as that of Medical Officer, Squadron Leader David Leaf, urging me to move. But where was I and why was he calling me darling? He knows my name. Through the fogginess I thought to myself, 'I'm alive! We crashed and I'm alive but, oh my God, my back hurts.'

'Come on, darling, you can do it.' I could feel him unfastening my seatbelt. I was attempting to take stock — oh my God, my back and my left hip hurt.

'I'm undoing your seatbelt. Come on, darling, we have to get out.' Why does he keep calling me that? Where is my left leg? Why can't I move it?

I could taste blood as my tongue located my lower left molars in the centre of my mouth. That's not right. I could feel that my teeth were not loose, so they should be to the side in my mouth, not in the centre. The acrid smell of aviation fuel hung heavy in the air and my flying suit was wet with it. I didn't understand why I was soaked in fuel but I didn't like it. My mind seemed to be attempting to process so much all at once. I was trying to fill a gap of nothingness; the yearning for an unwanted sleep that I could not shake off. It was clear that the helicopter had crashed, as I had feared, and that I had not died, as I had expected. The scream of the helicopter's transmission, now in its death throes, accentuated the fearful smell of fuel and I realized that we had only just hit the ground. We had crashed; I was alive and now I had to get out.

'I can't.' There was something horribly wrong with my spine, the pain ripped through my body and my left leg refused to move.

'Yes you can, darling. Come on we have to get out of here.' I felt the doctor's arm around my torso pulling me upward. The aircraft was lying on its left-hand side and what was once right was now up. I couldn't see anything, though I could feel that the bench seat upon which I had been sitting, and to which I had been secured by a lap-sash seatbelt, was now beside me to my right. With trembling hands, I could feel that the seat's frame created a ladder. I was still in the dark, but I could feel that the doctor was with me, right beside me, helping me.

Using the makeshift ladder and with the support of the doctor, I climbed to the door in excruciating pain. Reaching the top, I paused. The screaming engines and transmission added to the confusion as I sat atop the wreckage. I was wearing my flying helmet and I realized that the sun visor was down. This was not unusual for flying during the day, but it explained why it had been so hard to see anything within the wreckage. Flicking the visor up, I sat on the right-hand door of the helicopter and surveyed the underbelly of the aircraft, searching for any potential pathway to the safety of the ground. The skids of the helicopter were missing and I didn't stop to think why, merely noting that they were gone.

With the world filled with light again I emerged from my visual darkness, but the auditory hell still enveloped me as the tortured engines screamed out through the teeming rain. I could see that we had come to rest in a small clearing surrounded by trees, yet we were not far from what I recognized to be Timorese buildings. I had no idea where I was. I had not been to the village of Same before, so I wasn't even sure that that was where I was now. I had no real idea of how far we were from Dili, except for the vague and fuzzy recollection of the flight we had taken to get here. Would anyone be able to find us? One thing I did know for sure was that I didn't want to be here, wherever here was.

My body seemed to quiver, moving in slow and stilted motions and racked by a deep and central pain that seemed to radiate from my core — somewhere within my lower back and yet through every bodily fibre all at once. I felt that something was loose in my blood-filled mouth and so I spat into the palm of my hand, expecting a tooth but instead finding a piece of blood-stained chewing gum. A relief, even if minor.

I flung the chewing gum over the edge of the aircraft, down to the ground below, and immediately felt guilty for it. I had always taught the orphans of Dalam Asrama that they should not litter, that East Timor was now their country and that it was something they should be proud to cherish and protect. Despite having just survived a serious life-threatening accident, I felt guilt at being a poor role model for the children of this country by littering at the site of a helicopter crash!

'You need to get down. You have to get down,' Squadron Leader Leaf urged me.

'But how?' I asked. The underbelly of the aircraft was smooth but for two metal rods of the step jutting out at a precarious angle. It would be easy enough to slide down to the ground but those rods could do some serious damage and I felt I was already in a bad way. Thud! There was no longer any need to make a decision. My broken body fell through the air for the second time that day, slamming me face first into the mud. Squadron Leader Leaf had pushed me from the aircraft. Pain coursed through my body with the jolt, and I thought to myself this couldn't be happening, not to me. My disbelief persisted alongside an intense desire to just not be where I was, doing what I was doing.

Now I was starting to become acutely aware of where I was. I began to think about what medical resources were around me and how long and through which arduous paths it would take me to reach each of them. I wished I didn't know. I felt completely and utterly alone. My heart ached for the nightmare to end and for me to wake from my afternoon slumber, still young, fit and healthy and innocent of such trauma. I pleaded that this not be reality. I worried that the remainder of the AME team in Dili would have heard the mayday by now and were preparing to put themselves in the same danger we had experienced. I was torn between desperately wanting to see their friendly faces and anxiously wanting them to remain in the safety of Dili.

The doctor assisted me to stand and together we walked — or in my case, struggled, towards the village of Same. I urged him to leave me and return to the aircraft to find the boys. I hadn't seen them as I left the aircraft and knowing that the engines were still turning I was concerned for their welfare. I wondered where Greg was. He had been sitting by the right-hand door, so I should have seen him. We had exited through his door so he obviously wasn't in the aircraft anymore. But where was he? Squadron Leader Leaf didn't seem to know either, or perhaps he just wasn't letting on. He was determined to get me to shelter, but the pain in my back and my left leg was willing me to just lie down.

'Well, you'll get to go home now,' he told me.

'But I don't want to go home. I haven't completed my mission,' I replied. We were to be the final Air Force AME team in East Timor. This was a significant milestone in the recent history of Australia's assistance to the United Nations in East Timor. I had been a part of the first UN mission in 2000 and I had contributed to the planning of our withdrawal, here in 2004. That plan included me. How could I go home without having played my part? I continued into the first local home alongside the doctor, to satisfy his need to shelter me and feel comfortable to leave me to go find the others. We walked into what appeared to be a fairly rudimentary local house of mud walls and dirt floor, which, strikingly, did not appear to contain any furniture.

The doctor assisted me sit on the dirt floor and to remove my helmet. He lay me down and a group of East Timorese now appeared around us and placed a cloth under my head. I thought that it smelt of fuel but later, upon reflection, I concluded that that was actually me. I guess that once I was sheltered from the wind and rain I became more aware of the smell that had been there all along. Having settled me on the floor, the doctor left me there, alone, and went to find the others, as I had wanted him to.

I lay on the ground surrounded by concerned locals. I recall that although we were now indoors they held their umbrellas over me as if to shelter me from any further harm. Lying on my back was almost unbearable. There was something digging into my spine, which I thought was the Leatherman multi-tool on my pistol belt. Little did I know it was my third lumbar (L3) vertebra, so far out of alignment with the rest of my spine that it was digging into the ground. I reached to adjust my pistol belt in an attempt to make myself more comfortable and as I did so, two East Timorese men leaned toward me to assist. Instinct caused me to yell, 'No', as I grabbed to secure my pistol.

They jumped back, alarmed by my response. I seemed to be rapidly losing control of my situation. I knew they were trying to help me, and I didn't feel threatened by these people at all, but I did feel alone and extremely vulnerable. The slightest movement caused incredible pain and yet my body seemed to be in as much pain if I remained still. I felt as if I were squirming within my own skin, trying to escape and yet having nowhere to go.

My mind was just as unsettled. I began to try to focus on the flow of information that would have followed our mayday call. I concentrated on each stage of communication as it travelled from my Australian and UN colleagues in Dili to my CO in Australia and then the Defence Community Organisation, my family, my partner and the wider Air Force and Defence Force community. I felt guilty for having ruined their day. Surely it was almost time for dinner. It was time to put the working day to rest and to begin the slow wind down to the evening meal in the company of family and friends. It wasn't a good time for them to have to deal with an emergency — not here in Same, nor anywhere else in my life.

I heard a vehicle arrive at the front door of the house and its engine kept idling. The Timorese seemed to be hastily discussing something, which I could only assume involved telling the story of their extraordinary experience that afternoon. A Timorese man quietly kneeled beside me, and in the gentlest and most compassionate manner, placed his hand upon my shoulder.

'Missus, hospital,' he told me. A second man kneeled opposite him and began to lift my other shoulder to sit me up. The pain of movement struck me harder than ever as I struggled and stammered in reply.

'Yes, hospital.' Of course I would have to go to hospital. Their concern and their attempt to communicate with me was touching, but any form of movement was unbearably painful.

'Missus, hospital!' His words were more pleading this time as he too attempted to sit me upright. Were they trying to move me? What had changed that we now needed to move? Lying still had been painful enough, but this movement was unbearable, and yet I lacked the strength to oppose it. For people of such small stature they were strong enough to pull me upright and I could now see the white ute parked at the front door, the engine still idling.

'No! No, hospital. Australian doctor,' I pleaded. 'Doctor Australie!' I appealed to them in my best possible Timorese accent. I wished then that I had a more useful grasp of the local language as they dragged me through the house towards the front door and the waiting vehicle. I began to panic. The loneliness I felt reached a new depth as I imagined the terror that lay ahead. The only hospital I was aware of was two hours away in Dili, some 134 kilometres along what I imagined would be a mountainous, unsealed road. The only available place for me in this vehicle would be the tray and I was certain that there would be no cushioning involved. If I were to leave here, how would my team find me? Where were they? Why had they left me alone? I could not fight with these people, yet I did not want to go with them. My last-ditch stand of defiance came as we emerged from the house onto the front porch. The rain continued to fall and I summoned my remaining ounce of strength to once more succumb to the forces of gravity that day, slumping down into the mud out of the grasp of my handlers.

'No hospital! Doctor Australie!' I felt the tears rise in my throat, 'I can't go, they will come and get me. I can't go.' I knew that they could not understand my words but they seemed to appreciate my distress. With sighs of exasperation and more conversation in Tetum, we were on the move again. Grabbing me under the arms once more, they dragged me back into the house and back to my room where they lay me down and waited with me. I closed my eyes and allowed my fatigued and broken body to slump to the floor. I knew that this horror was far from over but for now I just needed to rest.

Squadron Leader Leaf eventually returned and told me he had found a schoolhouse he wanted to use as a casualty clearing post; somewhere he could gather all the casualties to prepare them for evacuation to Dili. This prompted me to ask once more if he had found the boys. He seemed to have been gone for so long, which could have meant he had had trouble finding them, or that they had needed his help. He assured me that he had found them and that they were okay. Again I asked after Greg in particular. He had been in the back of the aircraft with us and I was sure that I had some memory of him sitting beside the open door.

Squadron Leader Leaf reassured me that he was okay but that he thought he might have a fractured femur. I knew that that was not good at any time, but particularly in an area as remote as this. He could easily bleed out before receiving the surgery he would require. The doctor lifted me under my arms as two East Timorese men each took one of my legs and carried me across the road to the schoolhouse. I tried not to scream in pain and I can't recall if I did. But that journey was agonizing.

I don't remember much about the schoolhouse, except that children were still in the classroom standing alongside their desks. I felt concern that they were in the middle of this drama. I was once more laid down on the floor and Greg was brought in and laid down alongside me. I could tell he was drifting in and out of consciousness and I felt useless at a time when my colleagues, both doctor and patient, needed me most.

The pilots were in the room now and it was comforting to hear their voices and know they were alive. It required too much effort to lift my head to look at them so I just lay still and listened. The senior pilot was pacing backward and forward making a simple, yet repetitive apology: 'I'm sorry, I'm so sorry.' His words sounded like a mantra as I guess he tried to understand what had happened. His colleague sat to one side of me, gently patting me on the back and reassuring me that it was going to be okay. I should have been lying on my back but it was more comfortable on my front. I felt such sorrow for them both. We had all just set out to do a job. I didn't know what had happened and I certainly didn't feel any anger or blame towards anyone. I just wanted to turn back time, to be back at the Hotel Esplanada with the boys, enjoying Sunday brunch on the deck or a refreshing dip in the pool. I didn't want to be here and I certainly didn't want any of us to be hurting as much as we all were. Thankfully, they had seemed to have escaped any serious injury, just bruising and cuts.

We were eventually evacuated out of Same alongside the local East Timorese woman for whom we had launched our AME that day. I was relieved to know that she had not been forgotten in the chaos, and later learned that fellow Nursing Officer Flying Officer Higgins had remained by her side. Greg was loaded into a UN Bell 212 helicopter and taken directly to the UNMILHOSP in Dili. The East Timorese woman and I were being loaded into a Russian Mi-8 helicopter, which would be too large to land at the hospital, so we would be flown to the heliport on the outskirts of Dili and then transferred to the UNMILHOSP by road ambulance.

The Mi-8 was not fitted with any night-flying capability, and I believe that we were lucky to have been evacuated at all. Apparently the Russian pilots made a stance, reminding the team of the failing light and threatening to leave with or without us, as getting us onto the helicopter was taking some time. I understand the threat was met head-on by three defiant Air Force women — the healthy remainder of our team: Squadron Leader Sharon Sykes, Flying Officer Sharon Higgins and

Corporal Maria Brown. They were not leaving without us. Maria stood with a foot on the rear ramp of the helicopter and the other on the ground until she was certain we were all safely onboard. I'm not sure if the Russians would have left without us, but I am grateful not to have been left to spend the night in the village. I reckon the locals were quite relieved to see us all leave, ensuring that their usually peaceful corner of the world was released from this momentary chaos.

The UN hospital in 2004 was more centrally located than the one in which I had served in 2000 and was being run by the Thai military. I had visited the hospital when I first arrived in Dili almost three months earlier, but I had viewed it from the perspective of a Registered Nurse who might have to deliver and/or collect patients from their care. I had never considered that I might one day be a patient within its walls.

As I was wheeled from the road ambulance and into the hospital, I was not able to determine exactly which room I was in. It made sense for me to be in the emergency room but I could not be certain of my whereabouts. The medical personnel surrounding my bed blocked most of my view and my focus was blurred from an inescapable cocktail of mental shock, morphine and horrendous pain. My hearing seemed to remain sharp yet my memory always fails to deliver any images of that time. Were my eyes closed or was my mind so overwhelmed with stimuli that pictures were not necessary?

The initial medical assessment revealed that I had sustained three mandibular fractures, a wedge compression fracture of L3 with a retropulsed bone fragment in my spinal canal and aviation fuel burns to my back. Greg, the rescue crewman, had a fractured pelvis complicated by an arterial bleed. It was extraordinary that he survived; not only the injury but also the time and distance he had travelled before the surgery upon which his life ultimately depended.

For years prior to that fateful day, I had believed that the ADF physical fitness tests were merely an arbitrary measure of fitness to meet recruiting and employment requirements. What I learned that day was that physical fitness may be the determining factor in whether you survive the rigours of service. Greg and I were both fit. Had we not been, then perhaps the immediate outcome and the ongoing legacy of our injuries would have been much worse. The pilots and the doctor suffered a variety of non-penetrating soft tissue injuries and cracked ribs, demonstrating that fitness was not as significant a factor in the outcome for individuals involved in a crash, but rather where you were seated — some may refer to that as luck.

As I lay in my bed mulling over the diagnoses I had received, I was visited by Air Force Nursing Officer Wing Commander Paula Ibbotson, the UN Aeromedical Evacuation Operations Officer who was responsible for the co-ordination of AME flights.

She came to explain that Greg needed to be transported to Darwin urgently and that she had allocated the only AME aeroplane, the UN Dash-8 aircraft, for his transport. She also said that she was making arrangements for me to be flown directly to Brisbane the following morning with an Australian medical repatriation team and aircraft from CareFlight.

I was pleased to hear that Greg was heading home, but I didn't want to leave. Greg's injuries required urgent surgery and stabilization, so there was no question that he needed to be back in Australia as soon as possible. But I considered that all I required was a few days' rest in the UN Hospital and I would be able to return to work and to see out the mission. I had obviously not yet absorbed the severity of my own injuries. The Thais had some incredible surgical support with them and repairing my mandible wasn't going to be that hard, I thought. I needed to stay. Who would look after 'my nurses' if I were to leave?

'See you later, Coops,' Greg said as he left. His voice seemed so normal, so full of life, but I refused to answer him. I would not say goodbye and he would not die. Our AME team would deliver him swiftly to Darwin, where he would finally be safe. I just needed to continue my prayers for him until then. During that brief moment of irrational bargaining, Greg was taken away and I was left to berate myself for my silence. I had not said goodbye to him. Did I really think that such a foolish and childish deal would protect him? I was still out of control, imprisoned in my broken body, entirely reliant on those around me, and completely incapable of sorting my thoughts into some rational and useful order.

My next visitor was unexpected. It was my new CO, Lieutenant Colonel Nick Bartels. As we were flying to Same, and ultimately ruining the day for many, I had forgotten that the Australian CO in East Timor, Lieutenant Colonel Ross Bradford, was handing over his roles and responsibilities to his successor. It was not until the new CO stood beside my bed and introduced himself that I remembered he was a colleague of Conway's.

'Welcome to Timor, Sir,' I said, remembering Conway's explicit direction to me to remind Lieutenant Colonel Bartels of Conway and of Conway's best mate Lachlan. I had always expected that that conversation would have occurred over a meal in the dining hall and that it would have led to some interesting tales of Conway and Lachlan's exploits as young bachelor, Black Hawk helicopter pilots. He looked shocked and I instantly felt sorry for him. What a dreadful situation to be confronted with as you took command of a military operation overseas. It is such an honour to be appointed to a command role in the ADF, and even more so to operational command of deployed personnel. Yet the greatest stress of such an appointment is the responsibility to ensure that those personnel remained safe and returned home to their loved ones. There had not been a failure of military command on that day, and yet the incoming and outgoing COs were confronted with the serious injury of someone for whom they were responsible — me.

I put on my brave, albeit broken, face for them. They asked me if there was anything they could do for me or if there was anyone I would like to call. I thought of my parents, and of Conway. I wanted them to know that I was safe and I knew that this was best achieved by letting them hear my voice. I couldn't be sure that the system had managed to notify them yet and I was concerned about the impact the news would have on Mum. I trusted that my higher chain of command would be delicate and appropriate in their notification. I had made a note in my deployment paperwork that Mum was terminally ill and that any bad news should be communicated to my father. In response to the CO's question, I asked if I could speak to Conway.

'Of course you can, what's his number?' Lieutenant Colonel Bartels pulled out his mobile phone, ready and eager to do something to help. His number? His number? I knew it, it was in my brain here somewhere, but how could I forget his number? It was as if I were systematically rifling through a filing cabinet looking for the paper on which I had written it. When I found the paper in my mind my next challenge was to read the print. It took some time, and I'm sure that I announced each individual digit like a bumbling idiot as I dredged them from my foggy memory, but finally the CO was able to dial the number for me.

Conway's voice was as clear and calm as it had been earlier that day, so much so that I panicked that he had not been informed of the accident and I was now somehow going to have to find the right words to explain the adventures of my day. He reassured me that he knew of the accident and of the plans to get me to Brisbane the following day. I asked him to call my parents and to reassure them that I was okay. I wanted Conway to let them know that he had spoken to me and that I sounded fine. I was rapidly succumbing to the fatigue of the day and I was not confident that I could speak with my mother and maintain my brave facade.

I also asked Conway to call Lara and another of my close friends, to again ensure that the news was delivered sensitively. They were also officers within the ADF, and I knew that it would not be long before they heard the news through the ADF grapevine or possibly even via the media. Through Conway, I was beginning to regain some control of the situation. I thanked him, apologized for the drama of my day and reminded him of how much I loved him before saying goodbye.

The only other person I urgently wanted to speak with at that time was Gabi. Unfortunately, her phone number was saved in my mobile phone, which I had turned off prior to boarding the helicopter that afternoon and, try as I might, I could not remember the PIN required to unlock it. I did not know any other way of contacting her and feared I would not see her or get to reassure her that I was okay before I would have to return to Australia. My team members reassured me that they would find her and let her know what had happened. They would also provide her with my Australian contact details. It was the best that could be done but it broke my heart that I was leaving my little sister in East Timor without the chance to see her again.

I was exhausted. I had not been on my own since the evacuation from Same, with members of the Thai health staff and my own AME team members providing a constant stream of company beside my bed. Two of the AME team had left for Darwin with Greg, and those of the wider Australian team that were left agreed it was time that I was left to rest. I did not know what time it was, except that it was evening. My fellow Air Force Nursing Officer, Flying Officer Sharon 'Henry' Higgins, sat beside my bed, vowing to stay with me throughout the night. We had known each other for less than three months, yet we had quickly become such good friends.

I desperately did not want to be left alone, but I also knew that those around me had worked hard to save us that day and that they too were tired. I was concerned for them and I didn't want to ask for anyone to stay any longer than necessary. Henry didn't need to be asked, she just stayed. Still, the gut-wrenching feeling of loneliness and isolation that I had felt as I lay on the dirt floor of the house in Same stirred somewhere deep inside me. The intense fear that I had felt as we crashed had eased when I arrived at the UNMILHOSP, where I felt safe and secure once more, but the threat of loneliness persisted. Perhaps it was more a sense of vulnerability than loneliness, but all I knew in those early hours was that I did not like the intensity of emotion that seemed to arise only when I was alone.

Looking back now, I think I was beginning to realize that I had suddenly become significantly different to those within my peer group and that I had no idea where this unexpected turn would lead. I knew that my fitness was crucial to all aspects of my life, but specifically it was vital to my ongoing employment within the Air Force and as a Registered Nurse. But at that time I don't think I was consciously thinking of the consequences of my injuries. I was aware that everything had suddenly changed but I was not yet aware of exactly how. Life had just demonstrated how suddenly and unexpectedly it could change and what little control I had to prevent it. Perhaps I was feeling an overwhelming insecurity. What was going to happen next?

The night was long and restless. Henry's nursing experience was primarily in critical care, which up until now I had found to be very impressive. Now, as I was confined to lying on my back with little ability to move, I unconsciously tended to cross my ankles, probably just to shift position. This simple movement resulted in Henry delivering a stern tap on my leg or my toes, reminding me that crossing my legs was bad for my heart! Additionally, as a result of the nerve compression that was occurring in my spine, my left quadriceps muscle kept going into an uncontrollable and irritating spasm. I asked Henry to request a dose of Valium from the Thai nursing staff to stop the muscle spasm and to help me to sleep. Their incredulous response was that they could not recommend such a drug, as it was very addictive. We knew that.

Seeing my desperation, Henry tried once more and finally returned with the dose of Valium I had requested. It worked on my muscle spasm as I had expected it would and it was the only dose that I have ever had in my life. Sleep continued to remain elusive though. Whenever I closed my eyes and began to rest, I was jolted awake by the terrifying sensation of falling through the air. My heart would race, my breathing increased and my body trembled with fear as if I was crashing all over again. The night was as long as it was restless.

With the dawning of a new day came a new adventure. I was to be transferred from Dili to Brisbane in the CareFlight Learjet. I was anxious about the pain the trip might bring but received a continuous intravenous infusion of morphine and midazolam, which ensured I slept all the way home. I was transferred by road ambulance to the Dili airport, where I was surprised to be greeted by a large group of well-wishers. I felt a little overwhelmed by the presence of so many people, including my AME team, other members of the Australian contingent and the Thai health team, my CO, Lieutenant-Colonel Ross Bradford, and, unexpectedly, the UN head of the mission in East Timor, Sukehiro Hasegawa.

The sun blinded me, so Colonel Bradford promptly placed his sunglasses over my eyes, staying beside me until I was safely onboard the aircraft. I bade farewell to my friends and colleagues and to East Timor. I remained anxious about leaving my team behind, but I had to acknowledge that I wasn't of any use to them now. My mission in East Timor was over. Would my mission in the Air Force now be over as well?

CHAPTER 6

BROKEN AND BANGED UP

2004

With each stage of my return to Australia, my loneliness started to move to a sense of safety and security. Immediately on meeting the CareFlight doctor and Registered Nurse I felt comfortable in their care. Then, as we touched down at the Brisbane airport and I was loaded into an Australian ambulance and driven along streets that had a familiar feel, I began to relax just a little as I started to finally feel I was home. At the Royal Brisbane Women's Hospital I was met by my CO, Wing Commander Michael Paterson; the Squadron Administration Officer, Flight Lieutenant Janice Cudmore, and a fellow Nursing Officer, Flight Lieutenant Paul McGinty. I grabbed the CO's hand and held on tight. I knew that I still had a long journey ahead of me, but in 24 hours I was back where I needed to be. Things weren't great and I was not in good condition but I was back with people that I knew would look after me while I could not. Satisfied that I was home and admitted to the emergency department in the RBWH, my colleagues headed home to their families and once more I was alone.

Conway, who was living in Townsville, was due to arrive in Brisbane the following morning. My parents had desperately wanted to travel to Brisbane to be with me but I reassured them that I would be well looked after in hospital and that I would need them after I was allowed to go home. The truth was that I was afraid of the impact the travel and the stress of seeing me would have on Mum. She was still undergoing chemotherapy so I was also very concerned about any infections she might be exposed to by visiting me in such a large hospital.

My injuries were verified by CT scan — a technology not yet available in East Timor. The senior Orthopaedic Registrar confirmed that the force of impact had crushed my L3 vertebra to 60 per cent of its original height, destroying the L2–3 and L3–4 discs and forcing out a fragment of bone to occupy 50 per cent of the adjacent spinal canal. The fracture resulted in a 15-degree kyphosis at the level of injury. This meant that where my spine should have a lumbar curve inward to the core of my body, it now curved outward. The change in structure of my L3 vertebra had caused my lumbar spine to collapse in on itself. The resulting nerve damage was causing a disruption to the nerve innervation of the L3 and L4 dermatomes — evident as weakness in my left quadriceps, pain in my left knee and loss of sensation in the area of skin below my left knee and on the inside aspect of my lower left leg. These changes had been apparent immediately after the crash as I struggled to leave the helicopter and walk away, but it was only now that I was beginning to clearly understand why in a clinical context.

The force of impact had also fractured my jaw in four places. The fracture that was most obvious to me was the one that had completely broken through the left-hand side of my jaw, allowing it to unnaturally shift so much that my lower left molars now sat in the middle of my mouth. The other three fractures were on the right side and extended down from the angle of my jaw. It appeared as if the front right edge of my chin had impacted with my left knee, although it is still hard to visualize just how it had occurred. The only clues to the exact mechanism of injury were a graze on the right-hand side of my chin and a small bruise below my left kneecap. Perhaps I hit the seat, or even another occupant of the cabin. Precisely what caused my facial fractures remains a mystery.

The Registrar told me I would need a full lumbar spinal fusion — two metal rods, one on each side of my lumbar spine would be bolted to the vertebrae, like scaffolding, to hold it stable. For the surgeon to be able to access and stabilize my fracture, he would need to make an incision along my spine and around the side of my body to my navel. The thought of the continued trauma to my body and the huge scar that would be left sickened and disappointed me, but there was little I could do about it. My jaw would also need to be repaired and held together by titanium plates and screws.

As I began to contemplate and absorb this news, the Air Force's most senior operational Medical Officer, the Officer Commanding Health Services Wing, Group Captain Amanda Dines, visited me. I told her what I knew about my injuries and we reminisced about how concerned I had been for Conway's safety when he had deployed to Iraq in 2003 during Operation Iraqi Freedom — as the Americans called it. We acknowledged that as healthcare professionals our tendency is to worry about the welfare of others and not of ourselves. My accident was an abrupt wakeup call for all who served within Defence Health. Group Captain Dines reassured me she would remain in contact and that I should not hesitate in contacting her if I needed to.

Soon after she left, I was 'parked' in the corridor awaiting a bed on the ward and spent a long Thursday night in a busy emergency department, being jostled by the passing swathes of human traffic. I could hear the medical banter of the staff, the din and chatter of concerned family visitors to other patients, the cries of the sick and hurt, and the uninviting language of drunken revellers fighting. I was surrounded by people, and yet I felt alone. I had always treasured my solitude but this feeling was new and it was different to anything I had ever felt before. Being alone now seemed to be painfully and closely related to the intense sensations of fear and vulnerability that I had survived the previous day.

I was transferred to the orthopaedic ward the following morning, Friday, 4 June 2004, where I shared a room with three other women. The first task for the RN appointed to care for me, was to give me a wash. I had been immobile for 36 hours and was completely incapable of caring for myself. The fact I had been soaked in aviation fuel had escaped everyone's notice. If it had been noticed, it just hadn't reached the top of the priority list in my care. The fuel-soaked flying suit I was recovered in had been replaced by a Thai military hospital gown, but my skin was not washed.

As pleasant as a warm wash was, it was too late to arrest the damage that the fuel had caused my skin. I endured a free chemical peel of my back and shoulders, with my skin flaking off for days afterward, leaving me excruciatingly itchy. This was quite an irritating addition to being confined to bed and unable to move. Fortunately, I did not develop any permanent or obvious scarring from my chemical burns but to this day I remain vigilant for any symptoms that may arise from that event in light of other similar incidents involving aviation fuel. As an Air Force nurse I am well aware how in some instances, such as the F1-11 'Deseal Reseal' program, former ADF members exposed to aviation fuel appear to suffer a greater incidence of fatal cancers.

During my wash, the RN enquired as to how I ended up at the Royal Women's Hospital in Brisbane. To my surprise my answers were being repeated by the lady in the bed beside mine who seemed to be so enthused by my story that she promptly picked up the telephone and started relating the adventures of the patient who had just arrived in the room. The nurse apologized and promptly gained permission from the senior nurse to move me to a private room. It was only just dawning on me that what I had been through might be of interest to others.

When Conway arrived he held my hand and smiled at me, as if it were any other day, and jokingly commented, 'You don't look that bad.' Years later, after his own involvement in a helicopter crash, he confessed to me that his most fearful thought during the crash was not of dying but surviving with the unimaginable pain of horrendous burns. That day I was just pleased to see him and to have him by my side. I knew that everything would be okay now. I would be able to handle whatever was to come, as long as Conway was with me. In the true fashion of our relationship, as two staunch military officers, I briefed him on everything that I knew, from the incident itself to final diagnoses and plans for treatment. Happily what I had told him about my spinal surgery was about to change.

Unbeknown to me, over the course of the morning I had become the subject of a more positive and wider discussion among the orthopaedic team. Conway was with me as I received a visit from the orthopaedic spinal surgeon, who informed us that the team had decided that I was a good candidate for a more conservative and non-surgical course of treatment. In addition to the clinical indications, their decision was based upon my age, my level of fitness and, most importantly, because I was a Registered Nurse and a military officer. Basically, they were confident that I would do as I was told. I liked the sound of their plan and I vowed to be a compliant patient. I would avoid lumbar spinal fusion and commence the proposed conservative treatment straight away, which began with me being confined to bed for eight days, unable to move more than my arms and head and wriggle my toes. The bonus was that by the time I started I had already completed one day of the proposed treatment, by just lying in bed. Nonetheless, these would be the longest and most frustrating days of my life.

'Just lying in bed' would quickly become hard work. At the time of the crash, I had been at the peak of my physical fitness, going for a run and visiting the gym each day. I was at my goal weight of 55 kilograms and had never felt so fit and strong at any other time in my life. Lying in bed with nothing more than some gentle physiotherapy exercises to do was a sudden and vast change of pace. I was bemused to hear the physiotherapist was impressed that I was actually doing my exercises. Apparently her other patients didn't. But I would do whatever I could to get out of that bed. Given that my movement was so restricted, all I could do was to draw my abdominal muscles towards my spine to begin to strengthen my core again, and I did.

When I had arrived at the hospital I was placed on the emergency theatre list to have my jaw repaired and was required to fast for surgery. I had not eaten since the time of the accident 36 hours before. So adding to my discomfort was a lack of food. The timing of my arrival had not been great, as it was in a busy hospital in a large city and I was competing with weekend trauma patients for a place in theatre. While I may have been uncomfortable, my condition was stable and my injuries were not life threatening, so I knew that there would be cases more urgent than mine. The fasting continued until a theatre and a surgical team was available, 72 hours after my injury. I was finally taken to theatre and had my jaw fixed internally with plates and screws. As I had spent many hours assisting with faciomaxillary (face and jaw) surgery as a young theatre nurse in Hobart, I understood what my surgery would involve and I was keen to finally get it done. I reassured Conway that I would only be away from my room for about two hours.

It felt strangely comfortable to be back in an operating theatre, despite the fact that I was the patient. It was an environment that was so familiar to me and it represented another step forward in my recovery. I was put to sleep in my bed, to spare me the agony of being moved onto the operating table and, as if no time had passed, I awoke in the Recovery

Room to the gentle sound of my name. I felt relieved that the operation was over. I felt relaxed and free of pain. It was a pleasant feeling that I had not enjoyed since my flight home. Then I began to cough. As I turned my head I noticed I was coughing up blood onto the white linen pillowslip. This didn't really concern me, as I had just had surgery in my mouth, so I was expecting a little blood. But the cough continued.

'I want a CVC and an art line!' came the urgent request from a male voice that was too close to my bed for my liking.

'I don't need those,' I thought to myself. 'They've got the wrong person.' I figured I must have been hearing the theatre staff attending to another patient. The drowsy nurse within me felt concerned for the stranger in need of such urgent care. I felt calm and peaceful, but that false calm may have simply been a result of the cocktail of anaesthetic drugs and painkillers in my system. I was the patient in need of urgent care. I was dying.

I suffered a respiratory arrest — I stopped breathing. My lungs had filled with fluid, a condition known as pulmonary oedema. The exact reason for this was unclear. Initially there was a concern that I had reacted to the anaesthetic, and then there was the possibility that I had suffered a pulmonary fat embolism, either as a result of the trauma or more specifically because a fat embolus had been released into my blood stream from the site of one of my bone fractures. This is common in long bone fractures, where a glob of fat released from the fracture can start to cause problems to the circulatory system. Regardless of the cause, I was successfully resuscitated in the Recovery Room and transferred to the ICU for observation.

I had left Conway in my room with the expectation that he would see me again within two hours. It was four hours later when a nurse, who Conway described as the 'world's slowest nurse', finally arrived and informed him that 'the doctor needs to speak with you', and then asked, 'Can you please follow me?' I expect that no matter how fast they walked, it would never have been fast enough for him. He later told me that he asked the nurse if I was all right, to which she just replied, 'The doctor needs to speak with you.' With little information and no idea of where he was headed, Conway braced himself to hear that I was dead.

I have a vague recollection of waking up in the ICU with a continuous positive airway pressure (CPAP) mask strapped to my face, forcing air into my lungs. It was not until that moment, when I was being gently informed of what had happened to me following my surgery, that I began to accept that perhaps the injuries I had suffered had been much . more than a horrendously painful inconvenience; they had been a serious threat to my life. It was obvious that I had survived a helicopter crash, but I hadn't honestly acknowledged the severity of my injuries until then, nor did I ever consider that there was any ongoing threat to my life. It now appeared there was.

I was determined to get out of that bed and restore my health and fitness, but my body was doing things I could barely influence, much less control. Now I was an ICU patient. Not a position in which any nurse wants to find themself. It wasn't the invasive lines that seemed to emerge from every conceivable part of my body that convinced me I was an ICU patient; it was being conscious enough to realize that all that separated me and my dignity from the rest of the world was a square of strategically placed white linen, covering just enough to maintain some decency but leaving enough of me exposed so that all the lines and tubes to which I was attached could easily be accessed and maintained, and therefore I could also be easily 'accessed' in an emergency. I remained in ICU for 48 hours before being declared fit for transfer back to the ward.

My spinal fracture was under treatment, my mandibular fractures had been repaired and my skin continued to itch and peel as a result of the chemical burns, but there remained one injury that could not be scanned nor easily fixed and of which nobody spoke. I had suffered a significant psychological trauma. I had experienced overwhelming fear and believed that I would die. I had suffered intense physical pain and a range of powerful emotions associated with my injuries, including vulnerability, isolation and grief. I had watched on, helpless, as a friend and colleague fought for his life beside me in a simple Timorese schoolhouse in a village in the jungle, now 3500 kilometres away. But my mind, nor my 'state of mind', never seemed to rate a mention during my stay in hospital. For the eight days that I was immobilized in bed I thought of little else but the crash. Every time I closed my eyes during the first 48 hours and began to drift off to sleep, I would wake with a start as I felt myself falling through the air.

During the nights in hospital I would wake up confused and disoriented, as I thought I was still in the UN Military Hospital in Dili. Whenever the Queensland Government rescue helicopter came in to land on the roof of the RBWH, my heart would begin to race before I even realized that it was a helicopter that I was hearing. The song by Redgum about Vietnam veterans — 'I Was Only 19' — came to mind, where a troubled veteran beseeches a doctor to explain 'why the Channel Seven chopper chills me to my feet', was now completely identifiable to me. The sound of the rotors changing as the pilots tried to fly away from the trees. The sound of the dying engines as I struggled to get out of the wreck. And the sound of the other AME choppers that came to get me as I lay in agony in the rain. They had all left their indelible audio signature in my mind. Now my echoic memory associated those sounds with fear and pain and helplessness. These were all normal early responses to the trauma I had experienced and yet they were difficult and frightening, particularly when I was alone and when it was dark.

Despite the apparent frustrations of my recovery, I was overwhelmed by the support I received from family and friends, in particular from my Air Force family. My room was filled with get-well cards and flowers. Lara could not travel to Brisbane to be with me but she sent ridiculous faxes each day to keep my spirits up. Reservist members of the Health

Services Wing, who now worked at the hospital, would call by and check up on my progress. As did the Orthopaedic Registrar, Dr Patrick Weinrauch, who was an Army Reservist and a close friend of Flight Lieutenant Paul McCarthy, a junior Medical Officer with whom I had worked at 3 Hospital. I had received phone calls from the most senior military officer in Australia, the Chief of the Defence Force (CDF), General Peter Cosgrove AC, MC and the Chief of Air Force (CAF), Air Marshal Angus Houston AO, AFC. Both expressed their concern for me, their appreciation of my service and their desire to visit me, which we arranged to do after my discharge from hospital.

General Cosgrove's call caused quite a stir on the ward as two of the nursing staff were undergraduate Nursing Officers, one from Army and one from Air Force. The story relayed to me was that, late one evening, a civilian nurse had answered the telephone to be greeted by General Cosgrove. My calls were being screened by the staff to ensure that I was not bothered unnecessarily, and as she was not impressed with the time of the call nor familiar with who or what exactly the CDF was. She had covered the hand piece of the phone and informed the Defence Nursing Officers that someone who was the 'CDF' was on the phone. They mocked her, not believing that her claim was true, and one of them took the phone from her. Apparently upon hearing CDF's voice, the young Nursing Officer braced up and barked, 'Yes, Sir!' before transferring the call to me. I wasn't there to verify the story but it gave me a good laugh and continued entertainment in my relationship with these young Nursing Officers during my stay. I was a little short on entertainment!

On the ninth day of my hospital admission I was finally allowed out of bed and introduced to the 'old lady' body that was now mine as I began to learn to walk again. The most difficult part of this stage of my recovery was not just realizing the extent of my injuries and the loss that I had experienced, but also the intense recall of the emotions that I had felt at the crash site. Standing upright for the first time perfectly mimicked the pain of my injury as it had been at the crash site. It terrified me all over again. The long road ahead was becoming evident.

While it was important that I stand and learn to walk, it was just as important that my spinal fracture continued to be held stable so that it could heal. To enable this, I was required to wear an external back brace known as an 'O' brace. It was a contraption made of metal, which was covered with padding and vinyl and securely fitted around my torso to provide external support to the fracture. This external support would allow the fracture to fuse naturally without surgical internal fixation, in much the same way as a plaster cast applied to a fractured long bone in the arm or leg. I would wear it for fifteen weeks and was only ever allowed to remove it when lying down. I hated that back brace. I even fantasized about the day when I could dispose of it via a ritual burning. But it did help to remind myself that I would soon be free of it, whereas I would never have been free of a surgical fusion.

I remained in hospital for two weeks, learning to walk and care for myself again before being allowed to return home under the close supervision of Conway. Three weeks later, a mere five weeks after the crash, Conway returned to work in Townsville and Mum and Dad arrived to stay with me for two weeks as I returned to work at RAAF Base Amberley. My Medical Employment Classification was downgraded from the top classification of MEC1 to MEC303, basically deeming me fit to only work half days within the health centre and unfit for pretty much everything else required of my role as a Nursing Officer, including deployment, training and travel. Many people were surprised by my early return to work, but I viewed it as an essential part of my recovery.

As a single person, that is to say, unmarried, my support network had been and predominantly still was my workplace. My friends outside the ADF worked during the day, so the alternative to returning to work was to remain at home alone and dwell upon what had occurred and what the future might hold. Yet I was already tired of my own company. Being back at work gave me a reason to get out of bed each day and as I had begun to fear for my career and for my future employment prospects, it helped me to feel less vulnerable and to give me a sense of belonging. The day that I returned to work, the greatest challenge was simply getting dressed. After getting my uniform on over my back brace and somehow managing to reach my feet to do up my boots I was exhausted. I thought, 'Right, that's enough for today,' but I got up and went in regardless.

I felt I needed to demonstrate to my friends and colleagues that I was okay. There had been a great deal of upset surrounding my accident, as healthcare workers generally don't get hurt in the course of their duties, not even in a military context. It was an incident that reminded ADF healthcare personnel of the risks they take in providing healthcare to those in need, the remote localities in which they serve, and ultimately that their jobs are inherently dangerous. It reminded me as a military Nursing Officer of how pertinent my training, my fitness and my attitude were and of how rapidly a well-trained emergency response team can be reduced to its individual constituents. Our perspective of employment within the ADF had shifted.

Nothing had been said about my ongoing employment within the ADF but that in itself was concerning. I didn't know what was next. I was desperately afraid of losing my job — one that I loved so dearly. For the eight days I lay in bed unable to move, I had plenty of time to think. I had spoken to my spinal surgeon about my future and he was very clear in telling me that my nursing career was over. He delivered this brutal blow with as much compassion as he could but I was shattered. I had worked hard to gain my nursing degree and even harder to ensure that I took those skills to help others. I had turned my life upside down to become an Air Force Nursing Officer but in doing so I had lost the very thing I had to offer the world — my nursing. It was devastating. I was only a young nurse and it was what I continued to want to do. I was happy to have survived but I had to come to terms with what I had survived with. I may have welcomed the feeling of steady ground when I emerged from the wreck of that helicopter but now that ground was shifting beneath my feet.

My clinical nursing career was over and I was concerned that my military career would end as well. I didn't want that to happen. I had already lost so much in such a short period of time. I was only 29 years old and I had lost my health and fitness. I had not yet married nor had my children. I had barely travelled. I had an injury that would never heal completely; an injury that would forever remain deformed — my crushed vertebra and the associated nerve damage could not be fixed nor replaced, nor could it be restored to what it had been prior to injury. The raised ridge of misaligned bones that now graced my lower back due to the kyphosis was a constant reminder — along with the pain. My surgeon referred to it as a 'Dowager's Hump', so at not yet 30 years of age I had the spine of an elderly lady. As the weeks went by, more and more people started to talk to me about whether I would be fit enough to serve in the military. Everyone's opinion, medical and otherwise, was that I would not.

As a fairly stubborn individual, I simply didn't accept that. I wasn't ready to give up anything else. I had managed to avoid surgery, so if I could do that, maybe I could do more than anyone expected.

I was realistic that as a survivor within the ADF, I would need to accept that military life continues on, with or without individual members. The need to secure Australia and its interests doesn't pause to allow an injured Nursing Officer time to catch up, nor does it wait for her to give permission to continue on without her. If I wanted to stay, the onus was on me. The ADF had not yet established its Rehabilitation Program to support members like me to stay. That would come some years later as the number of physical and psychological casualties from East Timor, Iraq and Afghanistan started to rise, by which point I may have already lost my fight to remain. My physiotherapist reassured me that I was making good progress and doing much better than most people with similar injuries and for whom she had previously provided care. I sat down with my CO and my military Medical Officer and told them that I wanted to do whatever was necessary to stay. It was quite simple in theory, but much more challenging in the context of my new reality — within twelve months of my MEC downgrade I would need to demonstrate that I was physically and psychologically able to meet the requirements of my employment as an Air Force Nursing Officer, or demonstrate considerable progress toward achieving this.

At my request, my CO co-ordinated and chaired a meeting of all persons involved in my care, including my treating Medical Officer, my immediate supervisor — the Senior Nursing Officer, Physiotherapist, Psychologist and Chaplain. I informed the gathering that it was my desire and intention to remain in the Air Force as a Nursing Officer and that I needed them to help me in compiling a plan to achieve this. My primary goal was to attain a level of health and fitness that would enable me to return to work full-time in my pre-injury role and to pass my annual physical fitness test. I acknowledged that my goals may be unattainable and that I was not asking them to achieve the unachievable. I simply wanted their support for the following twelve months and a chance to remain. I agreed that if, in a year's time, I was not able to attain my goals, then I would concede I was no longer fit to serve and at that time, I would graciously accept my medical discharge. They all agreed.

I had a reasonable idea of how to navigate the system and was more than capable of advocating for my needs, but I often pondered what this experience would be like for younger, less qualified ADF members who had no prior knowledge of the healthcare system. Did they have the same level of support that I had? From my experience, I was confident that those receiving care within Air Force Health did but I knew that I was in a uniquely fortunate position from which I could fight to stay. I worked hard with my self-made rehab team and returned to work full-time on light duties in December 2004. I shed my back brace for the first time soon after and made my first interstate trip to Tasmania to walk down the aisle with one of my dearest friends on her wedding day.

Despite having worn my back brace for almost five months, I would find that over the course of the twelve months following my injury, my kyphosis, or curvature of the spine, would gradually increase to 30 degrees. This change was a compelling indication for surgical spinal fusion, but I was extremely fortunate to have a spinal surgeon who gave as much credence to my capability and my symptoms as he did to my spectacular X-rays. We worked together, he trusting me and me complying with his every instruction so that I continued to avoid surgery. Unfortunately, the nerve damage affecting my left leg never improved. I always tried to remain optimistic, and thus celebrated that my nerve damage actually worked in my favour whenever I had my lower legs waxed — I could only feel half of the pain!

As I returned to my Nursing Officer role there were new challenges. I became conscious of my desire to want to protect my friends and to not let them deploy. Although rationally I knew that they had a job to do and it was one they loved, I now feared greatly for their safety. I felt a desire to wrap them all in cotton wool and send them home safely to their families. I did not want anyone to have to experience what I had. I had become hypervigilant around aircraft, which was tiresome when I was working on the country's largest Air Force base. Friends commented that I appeared to become aware that a helicopter was approaching much sooner than anyone else, kind of like Radar O'Reilly from *M*A*S*H*.

I knew that my experience of listening to aircraft flying had changed in an abnormal way, as the high-pitched roar of an F-111 jet flying overhead would leave me waiting for the sound of a collision or a crash. I arranged an appointment with an Air Force psychologist, who reassured me that my nightmares, flashbacks, hypervigilance and fear of flying were all normal early responses to a traumatic event. I understood that I now had a memory of what happens when an aircraft crashes, so it seemed quite normal to now be afraid of that occurring again. I undertook my own informal program of desensitization to flying by not allowing myself to avoid flying. If my job required it I would do it. I would never enjoy flying again, and I would never make it through a flight without imagining it ending in a crash and so planned my escape route from each aircraft. But, to me, that seemed perfectly logical.

I concluded what was the worst year of my life by making a submission to speak at the ADF Nurses' Forum in Canberra — an annual conference for ADF Nursing Officers and Medical Assistants. As deeply personal as it was, I wanted to share my experience with my health colleagues, in the hope that I could alert them to the dangers of their role and hopefully save them from what I had experienced. I also wanted to give them some insight and a better understanding of what is was like to be a survivor of trauma in the ADF. They were — and would be — integral to the journey of other ADF members who had experienced trauma and, while no one would follow my path exactly, they would each in their own way and in their own time learn to navigate their own path of survival.

I discussed my view that survival is more than just not dying in a helicopter crash; it's about continuing to live. I lost my life in a single moment in the East Timorese village of Same. My life as I knew it was gone. I had had to pick up the broken body that was now mine, combined with a host of sad and frightening memories, and do whatever I could to move on. I started to learn how to live with this new me. The standing ovation that I received from my military nursing colleagues at that forum in Canberra represented the tide of support that had made my struggle that much easier.

Invigorated by my achievements I powered on, headstrong enough to begin planning a holiday in the United States and France for four weeks. I was tired of sitting still and I wanted to live, to enjoy my life in its entirety. Conway was scheduled to return to the US Army's Fort Lewis in February to undertake annual Chinook helicopter simulator training, so we planned for me to accompany him and for us to enjoy a holiday in France afterward. A temporary break from our usual life was certainly what we needed at that point.

While I was fit enough to enjoy the relaxed travel of a personal holiday, I was still far from being fit enough to travel and deploy with the ADF. This became starkly apparent on 26 December, Boxing Day, in 2004, when a sub-ocean earthquake measuring 9 on the Richter Scale sent countless billions of litres of water on an expanding journey across the Indian Ocean. When those waves reached shorelines they had towered into huge walls of water that proceeded to destroy everything in their path. The common term used to describe these events was tidal waves, but such was the impact of this event that its correct name — a tsunami — really entered the vocabulary of the wider public after it became the worst natural disaster in living memory. A quarter of a million people in a dozen countries lost their lives in that single event, which occurred in less than a day. In Australia it was labelled 'The Boxing Day Tsunami'.

Prime Minister John Howard was the first world leader to offer support and assistance to Indonesia, the country most affected, and immediately delegated the task of providing assistance to the ADF. Hundreds of ADF members were recalled from their Christmas leave to start planning and preparing to operate their planes, ships and helicopters as part of Australia's response. In the past I would instantly have been recalled for deployment, but I was not deemed fit enough for this mission and I understood that. But it was hard to watch my colleagues swing into action while I didn't even rate a seat on the bench on the sideline. I was firmly in the grandstand, watching events unfold on the TV news, just like the rest of Australia. I would be cheering them on and yet watching with benign envy as they brought some element of relief to the hundreds of thousands now suffering. Life went on for me, however, and Conway still needed to get to the United States for training three weeks later. So, as we had planned, I left my colleagues to their honorable mission to accompany him.

CHAPTER 7

LOSING MUM, LOSING FRIENDS, LOSING HOPE

2005

I have at times in the past had premonitions of sad and painful events that would occur in my life. On the night that I separated from Conway I knew that I had not been myself. It was not me that he had left but this hysterical woman he could no longer recognize as his girlfriend. I was so intensely emotional and unable to control the depth of feeling in my heart and my head. Looking back, it was perhaps the phone conversation I had had with my father on my return to Australia that day that was plaguing me. Mum's condition was deteriorating but he was unable to explain how, let alone why. He sounded tired and deep down I already knew that Mum was nearing the end of her battle, nearing the end of her life. I needed Conway then more than I had ever needed anyone in my life and yet neither of us could recognize it. The more I pleaded with him to stay, the more determined he seemed to want to flee.

The eventful nature of my life during the short course of our relationship had been fatiguing for me, and now it seemed that it had finally taken its toll on Conway. He had simply had enough and our relationship fractured under the intensity of the pressure. His facial expression, his posture, his pace, his tone of voice, all clearly showed his exhaustion. He had stood beside me until it was simply too hard to stand there anymore, and I think that what aggrieved me so acutely was that I could not follow and simply walk away from myself.

I felt empty. My back ached from the hours of travel on holidays and every cell within me felt battered by the emotional warfare I had engaged in with Conway. I laid down on the couch. The battlefield had fallen silent. No more discussions or arguments or desperate pleas, just a calming peace. My eyes rested on the scene through a high window on the lounge room wall. I could see the tops of a group of gum trees dancing in the breeze. Without any sound they appeared graceful, cast against the expanse of blue sky beyond. It was a scene that at any other time would not have even caught my attention but in that moment seemed to settle my soul so powerfully. It felt so tranquil in comparison to the intensity of the storm that preceded it. Even as the tears rolled down my face, I was captivated by the serenity of nature dancing before me. I closed my eyes capturing the image before time stole it away.

I did not want to die but I needed time to stand still until I could gain the strength to continue. The simple passage of time in my life had become a chore, yet there was no pause at any time to allow me to address it. It just marched on and as I struggled to keep up it dragged me along, battering me against the edges of existence, seemingly attempting to maim, kill or, at the very least, harden me. There was no negotiation of terms. Life had to continue on. Work didn't slow down, nor did the lives of my family and friends, nor the laborious monotony of the daily responsibilities of paying bills, maintaining my home and, as hard as it had become, of caring for myself. Time marched on and I struggled to keep up.

Some people might choose to blame my military service as the root cause of the breakdown of the relationship I had when I first joined the Air Force and they would be wrong. It ended for many complex reasons. But the end of my relationship with Conway was definitely as a result of my service. My service had broken me; it had changed me. I was certainly not the person I had been when Conway and I began dating. I acknowledged the physical change that I had endured almost immediately during the early days following the crash. I had even given Conway permission to leave if he wanted to. He chose to stay. I would joke that it was out of curiosity to see what I would do next, but that was then. Now our relationship had just become another military statistic.

I returned to work and blamed my dour mood on my jet lag. I refused to confide in anyone that I had failed once more in holding my life together and that Conway had left me. I could not bear to burden my friends with yet another 'Sharon tragedy'. I would hold it together for them. How could I inspire others by falling apart? They were so buoyed by my ability to face my adversity head-on and I would not disappoint them by falling apart now. I consulted one of the young Air Force Medical Officers, complaining of exhaustion and an unexplained rash that covered my body. I told him I had suffered from glandular fever during my university days and that perhaps he should take some blood and confirm that this was what was plaguing me now. He reassured me that I was merely jet lagged and probably suffering a contact dermatitis. He was one of many who would, like me, fail to recognize my depression. My facade was too good.

I was summoned to the CO's office and asked to explain why I had left the country without first informing my terminally ill mother. Such behaviour was certainly unbecoming of an officer of the Royal Australian Air Force, regardless of the extent of any recent trauma. I was dumbfounded. During my period of leave, the Base Chaplain had visited the CO to express his concern regarding a desperate phone call that he had received from my mother. She was deeply distressed that she could not contact me and she did not know where I was. That Mum would make such a call simply didn't make sense to me. I had spoken to her before I left, during my time away and again upon my return home.

Since Mum's diagnosis, whenever there was a chance that I would be a significant distance away from Hobart or even just out of contact for a day, I would call her to ensure that she was comfortable with my plans and that she did not need me to be at home with her at any time during that period. My chain of command was well aware of Mum's condition and they always ensured that any change in my circumstances was appropriate for myself and for my family at that time. I was fortunate to work for and with healthcare professionals who understood as well as I did the consequences of my mother's diagnosis. What Mum wanted for me most of all was to 'go out and live your life to the fullest, while you still can'. She only ever had one condition: 'Just make sure you send me a postcard.' I reassured the CO that I had not become a heartless bitch, and that he could reassure the Chaplain that I would contact home to make sure that everything was okay. The CO and I agreed that Mum's actions were out of character and that they could be an indication that something had changed, something of which I was obviously unaware.

At the weekend Dad called again. This time his frustration had subsided only to be replaced by an innocent desperation in his voice.

'Sharon, if you want to see your mother again, you need to come home.'

'Dad, what do you mean? What's happened?'

'I've had Dr Simpson to see your mother and he says she's terminal, she's not going to make it.' He seemed shocked, completely stunned by the news that his wife, my mother, was dying. I was confused. I knew my mother's cancer would end her life. She knew this herself and had discussed her fear of the end with me on long phone calls and on my visits home. I knew that she had not been able to get my sisters to have such frank and open discussions about her death. It was too painful for them to consider that she would not survive. Her love for my father and her desperation to not be parted from him compelled her to protect him from such a conversation and so no such conversation was ever had.

'Please, Dad, tell me what has happened? What's changed?'

He told me that Mum had been particularly unwell that evening, unable to stop vomiting and finding it increasingly difficult to breathe. He had been so concerned about her that he had called their local doctor to visit her at home. It was during this visit that the doctor was directly honest with Dad about my mother's prognosis. With the ever-decreasing amount of time that my parents would now have left together, Dad needed to know the reality of Mum's condition in no uncertain terms. It was also exactly what I needed to know. I took leave from work, packed my bags and headed back to the airport. It was a trip I had always known I would have to make and yet one I knew I would never be prepared for.

I was a nurse. My mother was a nurse. We had each experienced death at the bedside of others for whom we cared. For me, it had always been in caring for strangers, for people who were patients in my care. For Mum, it had also been for those for whom she had the greatest love. She had cared for her brother, her best friend, her uncle, her mother and her grandmother. With the greatest compassion she would do all that she could to bring peace and ease to them as they passed through the final stages of their lives. She possessed the exceptional ability to do this while maintaining the professionalism required of her position. Remarkably, even those whose behaviour would challenge her good Christian nature were those she regarded as needing it the most.

We each understood that as heart breaking as it was, it was also an incredible honour to be able to care for another as they prepared to die. This was the time when I had the skills and the knowledge to care for her and for my family in their greatest time of need, yet I had sacrificed my ability to do that. In the service of my country, and in the plight to save a much younger Timorese mother for the sake of her children, I could no longer care for my own mother in the way that I had planned to. I didn't blame anyone, but it was another stark reminder, another measure, of exactly what I had lost.

On 24 February 2005, my mother lost her five-year battle with breast cancer. I was by her side, along with my father, my three sisters and my eldest nephew. I did what I could to nurse her during her last days and to ensure that my family knew when they needed to speak their final words and when they needed to prepare themselves for her final breath. Finding the balance between being a nurse, a daughter to my father, a sister and an aunt, while at some point allowing myself to be a grieving daughter losing her mother, was something I did not achieve all that well. Some family members were concerned I was not displaying enough emotion, but how could I? Of my three sisters I had emerged as the 'strong' one. My parents needed me to be the foundation of our family, to ensure that as my mother left us and my father understandably wavered, our family would survive. Again, life wasn't allowing me time to catch up. I lost the greatest reference point in my life. But, still, as my mother had asked me to, I continued on.

I travelled back to Queensland and arrived home alone. I was finally in a space where I could mourn the passing of my mother, free from the responsibilities of her passing, free to just sit and cry and talk to her by myself. I was disturbed only by a gentle knock at the door. I opened it to see a car driving away and looked down to find the most beautiful bouquet of red roses on my doormat. The florist's card read: 'Dear Sharon, I love you. Conway.' We had spoken soon after Mum's death and agreed that our relationship had endured two significant challenges, including the geographical distance between us and the helicopter crash from which I had received such life-changing injuries. Yet we loved each other and resolved to try harder.

I returned to work once more, my mood now at its lowest ebb, despite the renewal of my relationship with Conway. I felt tired: physically, emotionally and psychologically. But still I knew that I must continue to work towards my goal of regaining my health and fitness so that I might remain in the Air Force. I continued my rehabilitation, feeling shell shocked yet determined. I was proud of what I had achieved and I thought that having lost my mum I was prepared for whatever may happen next. I was wrong.

I was beginning to feel like a valuable and contributing member of the Air Force once more and worked Easter as the acting Executive Officer — a military term for the second-in-command, of my unit. I received a call from the headquarters of HSW asking me for nominations for an AME team to deploy to Sumatra to work with the Royal Australian Navy. The region had been devastated by another massive earthquake similar to the one that triggered the Boxing Day Tsunami and the Australian Government was sending the ADF to provide yet further aid to the stricken region. The Navy had a ship — HMAS *Kanimbla* — on shore leave in Singapore after spending three months assisting the Indonesians after the tsunami. *Kanimbla's* crew were recalled from their break and the ship was being readied to head to the Indonesian island of Nias, only kilometres from the epicenter of both quakes. The AME team would fly by Air Force Hercules and rendezvous with the *Kanimbla*, using its embarked helicopters to provide medical assistance to the injured and displaced.

I scoured the list of available candidates and came up with the shortlist of health personnel who fitted the requirements of the mission. After various communications with headquarters I recalled Medical Assistant, Sergeant Wendy Jones, and offered her the opportunity to deploy on what would be called Operation Sumatra Assist II. She was excited by the opportunity. Wendy and I had been working together to organize a team for the Queensland Cancer Council's annual Relay for Life charity event. Wendy, of course, was doing most of the work, as I was busy trying to hold my life together. I jested that I would somehow get by without her, to which she laughed. Wendy was deployed on Operation Sumatra Assist II and I proceeded on leave. I travelled home to Tasmania to be with my dad for his birthday — the first since Mum had died.

It was hard to be home again. The reality of Mum's death was much more stark here. In Brisbane I could continue on, allowing my mind to think that she was still at home in Tassie. When I was in Tassie, however, I had no choice but to confront the fact that she was not there and that, despite the celebration of my father's birthday, my family was fractured by her absence. Dad was pleased to have me home. I assume that he liked having the company and I think he felt comforted by my presence. He had often described me as 'his rock'. Mum had been by his side for 35 years and now, five weeks after her death, he was still trying to find his way through the days without her. I had planned to spend a week at home with him but my plans quickly changed when I awoke on 2 April 2005. A Navy Sea King helicopter from HMAS *Kanimbla* had crashed on the Indonesian island of Nias.

I watched in disbelief at the TV news vision of the charred wreckage of the helicopter and the scorched earth that surrounded it. My heart raced as I wondered where Wendy was at that moment and with whom she had deployed. I felt sick. I called my team at work, and I called friends. I was desperate to hear that everyone got out alive. I was wanting to hear that Wendy was alive but during the early stages after the disaster the first priority was to notify families and care for them. I recall the moment when I was finally notified of the news that I did not want to hear. Nine ADF personnel had died. Miraculously, two had survived.

'Sharon, I'm sorry, but Wendy died.'

I had been standing in my parents' kitchen leaning back on the kitchen cabinets. My hand trembled as I managed to hold the phone to my ear but my body slid to the floor. Sergeant Wendy Jones had died. Alongside her was Air Force Medical Officer Squadron Leader Paul McCarthy and Nursing Officer Flight Lieutenant Lynne Rowbottom. It felt as if the world were closing in around me. I hung up the phone and just sat there on the floor. Tears rolled down my cheeks. I was conscious of my need to remain strong for Dad but I was numb. I felt defeated. I needed to dig deep to find the strength to stand up and face life once more. I needed to be with my Air Force family. I flew back to Amberley the following day and then on to Sydney for the first of many memorial ceremonies.

I stood at the edge of the airfield at Sydney airport and watched as nine flag-draped coffins were carried from the back of an Air Force C-130 Hercules. I watched on as grieving families touched the cold metal boxes that contained the remains of their loved ones. I thought of my own family and of the terror and pain that I had inflicted upon them as a result of my involvement in a helicopter crash. I chastised myself for having ever felt self-pity in relation to my own accident and I vowed that I would never allow myself to dwell in such self-indulgence ever again. I felt gratitude that my family had been spared the heartbreak that I now witnessed before me and yet incredible guilt for having survived.

For the most part of the ten months since my accident, I had felt as though I was attempting to pick myself up and brush myself off but the world was continually knocking me down again. At times I was struggling just to keep my head above water. I had endured more than most in a short period of time and some days it was not as easy to bear as others. Time, however, would not allow me to feel sorry for myself. If I stopped, I would drown, and that was not an option. I had survived and I had no right to squander that privilege. Nine of my colleagues had not survived, so this was no time for further self-pity.

The ADF began a period of significant introspection after this crash. Like another helicopter crash that occurred in 1996 in Townsville that killed friends of Conway, there was always a predictable course of events set in motion as investigation teams and enquiries are raised.

Conjecture and rumour and, inevitably, finger pointing commences as the cause of the accident is sought. As it turns out, the accident was caused by the lack of a split pin, a small piece of shaped wire designed to stop movement in another item. You could buy one at a hardware store for a few cents. Something as trivial as a piece of shaped wire spelled disaster for families and, less significantly, millions of dollars in the cost of the accident. Nine of my colleagues had perished and two survivors had been seriously injured for the lack of a small piece of shaped wire. Life was as vulnerable as it was precious. Those of us in Air Force Health continued on and commemorated our comrades as the Navy did theirs and I continued on with my rehab program with a greater sense of determination.

The clock was ticking and my twelve-month rehabilitation program was drawing to a close. With the tremendous support of my pre-injury running companion and dear friend, Nursing Officer, Flight Lieutenant Kay Wiseman, I passed my annual physical fitness test on Monday 11 July 2005. It was one month overdue, but I was medically fit to be upgraded to MEC202, which meant I could deploy on operations provided I had access to pharmaceutical pain relief. Because of my spinal fracture, I would never again attain the highest category of MEC1 — able to provide unrestricted service on deployment.

Passing my PFT was a significant milestone and a key indicator that I had the drive and determination required to salvage my ADF career. It was decided. I would continue to serve. With renewed vigour I set out to demolish every conceivable obstacle in my path, including returning to the air. On Tuesday 6 September 2005, I travelled to Toowoomba west of Amberley to take my first helicopter flight since the crash. Brigadier Tony Fraser, Commander of the Army's 16th Aviation Brigade, knew of my circumstances through his connection with Conway. As a pilot he understood how important my first flight would be in determining my future propensity to fly and, thus, my ability to continue to work as an AME nurse. So, acting on a request from Conway, he assigned a helicopter and crew for my use.

This would be the horse I would get back on to ensure I could still handle flying again. I flew in a Bell UH-1 Iroquois, colloquially known as a Huey. It was as close an aircraft as the ADF had to the one in which I had crashed. I was also allowed to choose a pilot I felt comfortable to fly with. The circumstances surrounding my first flight and the efforts of those involved ensured I was as supported as I could be for someone who was likely to be deathly afraid of being near or in a helicopter again. I discovered I loved to fly just as much as I ever had, but I also felt a tremendous sense of relief when I had my feet on the ground once more.

Then came the most momentous milestone of all. There had been yet another series of bombings in an area of Bali, which was popular with Western tourists. The first Bali bombing in 2002 had killed 202 people including 88 Australians, 38 Indonesians, 27 Britons and seven Americans, along with 48 victims from twenty other nations. There were also 209 injured in the two blasts at a local nightclub strip. Most of the survivors suffered horrific burns and had to be evacuated to Australian hospitals in Darwin and Perth by the Air Force and other emergency aviation agencies for treatment. The following year in 2003, the American JW Marriot Hotel in Jakarta, Indonesia's capital, was bombed with twelve injured. In 2004, the Australian Embassy in Jakarta was the site of another bombing, which claimed nine lives, all Indonesian, and injured more than 150. Now, in 2005, a second bombing in Bali was initiated by the terrorist group, Jamaah Islamiyah.

Reports were filtering in that scores of people had been killed and over a hundred were injured. The Air Force was requested to provide AME support to the evacuation of Australians. The whole country held its breath while news trickled in about the casualties from this latest tragedy, which the press would dub 'Bali 2'.

I received a phone call in the early hours of the morning, Sunday,

2 October 2005, from my headquarters asking if I was 'available to deploy'. Of course I was! Deployment was the ultimate achievement and culmination of all of the hard work I had put into my rehabilitation. I was appointed as OIC FAST, the very same position that had kept me from deploying on the response to the first Bali bombing in 2002, Operation Bali Assist. Before the sun was up, I was in the back of a taxi and on my way to Brisbane airport. I knew that this deployment would serve as a test of my ability to truly continue to serve as an Air Force Nursing Officer and I was determined that I would give myself every conceivable chance to succeed. This was just as much a test for me as for anyone in my hierarchy. I wasn't so determined to succeed that I would sacrifice even more of my health and fitness for my service but I was certainly working towards finding a balance.

By the time I arrived at the airport I was already in pain. One of the triggers of my back pain was travelling in cars. Being the driver myself was worse than as a passenger, as I could not shift position easily. But even much worse than that was the jarring stop/start driving technique of so many taxi drivers, and the occasional friend with whom I have driven. The taxi drive to Brisbane that day was no exception. Fortunately, there was time to rest at the airport before a very comfortable QANTAS flight to Darwin. From Darwin, as a member of the Air Force Health team, I boarded a C-130 Hercules transport aircraft alongside our medical equipment and supplies.

The organization, preparation and transport of casualties in Bali was textbook. A small team of Air Force Health personnel, commanded by senior Air Force Medical Officer, Wing Commander Steve Davis, had been flown in very soon after the first reports of the bombing. Its task was foremost to work alongside the Australian consulate personnel to identify casualties requiring aeromedical evacuation to Australia. Casualties began arriving via ambulance at the airport soon after we landed. My first impression was profound. These casualties were ordinary Australians, dressed as you might expect for a tropical holiday, mostly in shorts and T-shirts or light summer clothes. Yet here they were on stretchers with wounds and wound dressings more like that of battlefield soldiers.

The AME teams set to work to assess, treat and prepare them for their flights back to Australia and to hospitals close to their families. The mission did not restrict itself to Australian citizens, but to all casualties requiring AME to Australia. The FAST was not required, except for a few minor pieces of equipment, so I assisted the AME teams in their work. We introduced ourselves to our patients, explaining how we would prepare them for their flight home and care for them during the flight. We assessed wounds, checked dressings and intravenous lines and carried out a thorough medical assessment to ensure each patient was fit to fly.

I remember an Australian couple who were on holiday in Bali and who had both been injured while out at a café enjoying their dinner. They could well have been my parents. I recognized their relief in seeing Australian faces and hearing Australian voices. I understood their desperate desire to wake from the nightmare they were in, and their soul-wrenching ache to simply go home, to be surrounded by their loved ones once more and to feel safe. I recognized it all. I had felt it all. On that airfield, I discovered so many more benefits to this deployment than simply proving that I could deploy. I discovered a new ability within myself to relate to and care for the injured overseas, one that I had never contemplated before that moment, a maturity in my capability as an Air Force Nursing Officer. I was discovering that there were some benefits from my experience of being injured in a foreign land and wanting above all just to hear an Australian voice and to go home. I reassured them that they were safe and that they were on their way home.

With the patients safely aboard, the Hercules departed for home with their precious cargo. I stayed on in Bali overnight as part of a small team that might be needed if more casualties were identified or further requirement for AME of existing casualties was established. But the operation went so smoothly our additional services were not needed. We got everyone out quickly and efficiently and I returned home to Brisbane the following day. My first deployment since the helicopter crash was over. I had finally proven that I could still do the job that I loved — to myself more than anyone. My achievement was celebrated among my colleagues as I returned to work. They knew just how momentous this deployment had been for me and their pride in me was obvious. I owed them so much. I was back.

But as I forged ahead I would again be reminded of the dangers of helicopter flying. Later that year I was to receive another phone call that would make my heart race and my knees weak. It was Conway. Any other time it would be nice to hear his voice, but the first words he uttered shook me to my core.

'Shaz,' he said, 'I'm all right. I've had a helicopter crash but we all walked away.' It took me a few seconds to come back to earth.

'Shaz?' Did you hear what I said? I'm fine, we all walked away without a scratch.'

Conway had left the full-time Army and transferred to the Reserves earlier in the year and had started a civilian job flying small helicopters doing maintenance patrols along power lines. I did not like the type of work he did, especially when I saw a video of the tiny helicopter he was flying and how close he got to the power line — usually about three metres, with an electricity linesman standing on the skids inspecting the power poles and another sitting next to the pilot — Conway — typing a report into a small laptop. On this particular day he was patrolling a line from Toowoomba to Warwick, not too far from RAAF Base Amberley where I was stationed. I asked him for details, but in his usual understated way he merely said, 'I thought it was just my ham-fisted flying, but it seems we had a mechanical failure of the tail rotor. We spun around a few times and "spudded" in . . . but there's not too much damage and we're all okay.' It was then that he said something more disturbing.

'That's not the most exciting thing that happened to me today, though!'
Oh no! What now?

'What could be more exciting than crashing a helicopter?' I asked.

'The Office of the Chief of Army just called me as I was letting the authorities know I was all right. They asked if I could talk and I figured that the helicopter wasn't going anywhere, so I said yes. They have commissioned me as the Army's Official War Artist! I'm getting back into the Army and I'm off to Iraq and Afghanistan! How cool is that?'

Cool is not exactly the word I would use to describe the fact that my boyfriend, who had already done two tours of East Timor and one of the Middle East during Operation Iraqi Freedom, was now likely to be going back to war.

'I'll be the first Army artist since the Korean War!' he said excitedly. 'The civilian artists that are used have to be babysat and can't go anywhere. The Chief of Army wants me to be an Army artist and to get out and patrol with the infantry and capture the essence of the war from outside the wire!'

This was too much for me to bear. A chopper crash! A deployment to Iraq and Afghanistan patrolling with the infantry! Yes, Conway had been a graphic designer before becoming a helicopter pilot for the Army and had dabbled while in uniform – his pictures of aircraft and his portraits of soldiers had started to get such a following within the ADF that he became known to Army HQ as an artist of some skill. But I was still shaken by Conway's first words, that he had had a chopper crash.

It was only later that I heard the full story of the event. He was recounting the malfunction to his best friend Lachlan, also an Army pilot, who lived in Toowoomba, as they spoke pilot-to-pilot with plenty of technical jargon that may as well have been Greek to me. It seems that when the helicopter first started spinning out of control, the electricity linesman who was standing on the skid was flung out of the helicopter suspended by a metre-long strap. The linesman who was sitting in the seat next to Conway flung the computer to his feet and hung on. He had already been in two helicopter crashes, one had put him in hospital for three months, and he merely said, 'Get us on the fucking ground!' without panic, but with emphasis. It seems that the procedure for a tail-rotor failure is to 'chop the throttle' and 'autorotate' to the ground, which is pilot-speak for turning off the power and using whatever lift was left in the rotor system to cushion the crash.

It was then that Conway related to Lachlan that the reason he didn't do that was that he was directly above the power lines and trees, and doing so would have meant immediate electrocution or being turned upside down and crashing to earth. Instead he kept the power on and tried to manoeuvre into a clearing as he watched trees and sky spin in front of him in a blur of blue and green. I just sat there, stunned by the picture of a helicopter spinning out of control above power lines with a person outside it tethered to a strap being flung like a rag doll spinning on a Hills hoist while Conway tried to prevent it from descending into 11,000 volts and at the same time keeping it upright and airborne and guiding it to a hole in the trees.

As I sat quietly in my own private shock, what became more shocking was how excited he was at the idea of deploying to Iraq and Afghanistan as the Army's Official War Artist. All I could think was that, while he might be carrying a rifle, no matter how hard you try, a paintbrush doesn't shoot bullets too well if that's what you're carrying the moment they start flying.

CHAPTER 8

WORKING FOR THE MINISTER FOR DEFENCE

2005 to 2006

My service to my country had robbed me of my health and fitness before the age of 30. I had learned so dramatically how my career choice could end my life, but this was an accepted part of military service and a risk acknowledged by thousands of ADF personnel. What was more of an immediate threat was that the privilege to serve could be denied to me.

The brief return to Bali in 2005 proved that I had regained the required level of fitness to deploy. The next test was to deploy in support of an established and dedicated operation. I continued to test my level of fitness, mindful that it would be examined closely by those who had the power to limit my military future, especially if I failed. An opportunity arose to deploy to Balad in Iraq as a member of the third rotation of the Australian Medical Detachment in support of the United States Air

Force Hospital. Perioperative nurses were needed and, with my CO's endorsement, I nominated to deploy. Amid great excitement I was accepted. Many had said that it was not possible that I would deploy again, but I saw my name up on the operations board in black and white, and I was thrilled.

The time prior to deployment can be one of some anxiety as you begin to mentally prepare yourself for the task ahead. I had experienced this stage of deployment twice before and so, to my surprise, I recognized that rather than feeling those familiar nerves I felt relaxed. I had proven myself to the extent that my senior officers had regained their faith in my abilities as an Air Force nurse and a military officer, so much so they were prepared to once again treat me as an equal among my peers. Well at least that's what I thought.

Without explanation, my preliminary identification for deployment to Balad was cancelled. My name no longer appeared on the team list. When I enquired why, there was no explanation. I was still merely a Flight Lieutenant so I knew that my enquiries of HQ staff would have to end there, but I pursued the matter further with my CO. I expressed my concern that I had been replaced with personnel who were less experienced and thus the only explanation that I could see was a lack of faith in my abilities and my fitness to serve on a wartime operation.

He reassured me that the decision was not made as a judgement of my fitness to deploy. He had been my greatest support in my fight to stay and he knew just how important this next milestone was for me. I trusted that he was conveying what he had been told by HQ, but I didn't believe the 'party line' that he had been fed. I was shattered. I was frustrated. How much more did I need to do to prove myself? For how long would I be 'the Nursing Officer that survived the helicopter crash?' I had fought for my life; I had fought for my career; just how long was I going to have to fight to regain professional respect over pity and sympathy? I believed that despite jumping through the necessary hoops of Defence fitness requirements, I was being denied the opportunity that I wanted the most: to be an operational nurse again.

It was time for me to leave Defence Health. The only way I could once again be accepted for what I was able to do today — rather than what happened to me yesterday — was by removing myself from the company of those who knew about yesterday. It was a very difficult decision. My friends and colleagues had been by my side from the moment the first AME team arrived in Same. In leaving Defence Health I was leaving them, but they understood my plight and that this departure from their ranks was just the next step in my journey.

By chance, the position of Aide-de-Camp or ADC to the Chief of the Defence Force, Air Chief Marshal Angus Houston AO, AFC, arose. An ADC is a unique military role. Historically it is the senior aide to persons of high rank within the military or government. In order for an officer to be considered for the posting — which was only for twelve months due to the incredibly high workload — an officer needed to be considered by his or her chain of command as being suitable for representational duties by their professionalism and dress and bearing. The officer then needed to prove that they had, and I am quoting here from the Defence career management directorate, 'Well developed time management and staff skills; Excellent attention to detail; The ability to work harmoniously in a tri-service and civilian environment; and a preparedness to work long and irregular hours'. I discovered that no truer words were ever written, and yet they still did not adequately reflect the unique nature of the role.

I submitted my application, and was shortlisted and told to report for interview. I felt confident that I had a good chance. Having met the other applicants, I was the only one who actually wanted the job. The others were either pilots or navigators who had been selected and nominated in high recognition of their career performance and their potential to rise to the rank of Service Chief. It was a type of 'exposure posting' that would provide them with valuable insight into the higher headquarters of the organization. In that regard, I was out of the running. A Nursing Officer would never rise to the position of Chief of Air Force, and certainly not Chief of the Defence Force, nor should they, yet with my seniority and my experience I thought I had the job in the bag, and maybe I would have, if not for my crash.

The interview went so well that, afterwards, Air Chief Marshal Houston praised my high suitability for the position, and did so in front of the other applicants. He then told me as compassionately as he could that he had a duty of care to me and that with his knowledge of my injuries and of the requirements of the position, he was concerned that I would not cope physically. As the tone and content of his words went from praise to gentle but certain rejection my heart sank. Standing proud and tall in the manner expected of a military officer, it took every bit of strength for me not to crumble. I could feel the lump rising in my throat and tears welling in my eyes.

I did my best to feign sincerity in congratulating the officer who had been selected but all I wanted to do was to be released from this sense of humiliation and to find somewhere to shed a few private tears of disappointment. Angus Houston is one of humanity's true gentlemen. He is a man for whom I have always held the utmost respect and whose leadership style and ability I have always strived to emulate. I sincerely appreciated his care and concern but was nonetheless crushed. That damned crash had robbed me again.

The hits had just kept coming, losing Balad, now the ADC to the CDF! I had sacrificed so much for my career, my service, my country. I had worked so damned hard. Was I delusional? Was I kidding myself that I could remain? The message I was beginning to hear loud and clear was 'No, I could not.'

As the saying goes, when I thought I was being rejected, I was actually being redirected. This would prove to be the case. My career manager still had his job to do and still had ADC vacancies to fill if I was interested. He encouraged me to apply once more for the position of ADC to the Minister for Defence. At that time the Minister was Senator Robert Hill. Reluctant as I was to suffer another setback, I made my application, and was again shortlisted and interviewed. The Minister was not involved in the interview process, but his Chief of Staff, Personal Assistant and current ADC were. They were wonderful people and I became excited about the prospect of working with them. I was upfront about my injuries but they said they just needed to know that I wanted the job and was capable, qualified and suited to it. Apparently I was.

Finally, I got a little validation that I wasn't headed for the scrap heap just yet. Yay! Success! I was to be posted out of Air Force Health for twelve months, giving me the time and space I needed to reconsider my future career. It also meant I would need to relocate, so I packed up all of my possessions and headed for the nation's capital and my new office in Parliament House.

As I settled into my new apartment in Canberra, my attention was drawn to a TV news item. Two senators had just announced their resignations from parliament, including the Minister for Defence! Senator Robert Hill had tendered his resignation from Cabinet as Minister for Defence and intended to resign from the Senate and not contest the next election. My new boss, whom I had not yet met, was no longer my new boss.

A Cabinet reshuffle soon followed and it was announced that the Honourable Dr Brendan Nelson, Member for Bradfield, had been appointed as the new Minister for Defence. Dr Nelson was a former Tasmanian GP, who had served as the youngest ever National President of the Australian Medical Association. Elected to Parliament in 1996, he had served as the Parliamentary Secretary to the Minister for Defence, and subsequently as Minister for Education, Science and Training. Despite his high profile, I had very little knowledge of him. I was, though, struck by the irony that he was a doctor of medicine and that I was a Registered Nurse attempting to take a break from the health workforce.

I had not been employed to work for Dr Nelson, so he had every right to request a fresh round of candidates for the position of ADC. Fortunately for me, he did not deem that necessary. He wasn't yet sure why the position of Minister for Defence required an ADC, but he welcomed me to his newly evolving team. It seemed that together we would learn what it was that my role would involve.

Our first joint lesson was that he did not like to be called Sir, and that I had become so indoctrinated within Defence, that I found it difficult not to do so. He insisted that I call him Brendan, just as he requested of everyone he met. I responded by insisting that as a member of the ADF, it was not my privilege to call him Brendan and that I would always refer to him as Minister. It was a middle ground upon which we could both play the protocol game, although we were each probably not entirely happy with the outcome. We came to learn that if I stumbled and occasionally addressed him as Sir, it was a pretty good indicator that I was either tired, or that I differed in opinion on a matter under discussion.

The Minister also disliked the protocol that dictated that I should open his car door for him. He was uncomfortable with such privileges of status and position. His honest and very 'blokey' opinion was that it made him look like a 'wanker'. We agreed that such Defence-specific ceremonial protocol would only be observed on ceremonial occasions. On all other occasions he would defend me to my military hierarchy in the event that I was criticized for an omission of duty. They were trivial matters in the spectrum of his responsibilities, but to me they were an indication that he was a reasonable man and that we could work together.

The significance of my role and the opportunities that it would offer became starkly apparent on 27 January 2006. My first official duty was to accompany the Minister to Government House to attend the swearing in of the Federal Cabinet. I felt like a tourist in a whole new amazing and foreign world. There I was, in a car with the Minister for Defence, driving through the gates of the official residence of the Governor-General, Government House. Then, in the presence of the Governor-General — the Queen's Representative in Australia and Commander-in-Chief of the Australian Defence Force — I bore witness to the swearing in of each and every member of the Federal Cabinet. Not many Defence members are afforded such privilege in their careers.

Over the course of the year I would be present during the visits of foreign dignitaries to Parliament House, including the Prime Minister of New Zealand, Helen Clark; the UK Prime Minister, Tony Blair; the Prime Minister of Singapore, Lee Hsien Loong; the Prime Minister of Cambodia, Samdech Hun Sen; and, probably of most significance to me, the Prime Minister of East Timor, Dr José Ramos-Horta. I was also fortunate to meet a woman I had long admired for her intellect and her personal ambition, drive and achievement, US Secretary of State, Condoleezza Rice. As well, I met US Vice-President Dick Cheney in the West Wing of the White House, and US Secretary for Defence, Donald Rumsfeld, at the Pentagon, not far from the 'scorched stone'. This single stone stands as a memorial to the 184 people killed when a hijacked commercial airliner American Airlines Flight 77 was deliberately flown into the Pentagon on 11 September 2001. It was scorched by the impact and deliberately retained in the rebuilt wall to mark the point of impact and to commemorate those who had died.

It was like I was living an episode of *The West Wing* TV drama. These were some of the world's most powerful and influential politicians, who appeared regularly on Australian television, and I, a Registered Nurse from Hobart, would shake the hand of each of them. Every day as I drove toward my place of work — Parliament House in Canberra — I would gaze up at the huge Australian National Flag waving from atop the roof and remind myself just how incredibly fortunate I was.

The year ahead was peppered with similar unique and amazing events but the early days and weeks were consumed by a seemingly endless array of briefings for the Minister and his staff. Through this process those of us within the Department of Defence became acutely aware of the Minister's incredible desire for knowledge and his remarkable memory for detail. He was able to read and study a brief, make a few notes and then, with notes tucked securely inside the inner breast pocket of his jacket, stand before an audience of experts in the field and address and discuss the content of the brief as if it had been his life's work. Even the most intricate of technical detail didn't escape him.

Undoubtedly of greatest concern to some within the Department was that the most important detail that he remembered was the name of the author of the brief. If he had a question regarding the content of a brief, he would not call the service chief who had endorsed the brief but pick up the phone and make direct contact with the author. This didn't exactly comply with the chain-of-command requirement of communication within Defence, and it certainly shocked a few authors who answered their phone only to find themselves speaking directly to the Minister. I knew that if I informed the Minister of anything, I needed to be damned sure that I was right as there wasn't a snowball's chance in hell that he would forget who told him.

Despite my exciting new post, I was still required to meet and maintain the level of readiness and fitness demanded of me as a Defence member. My spinal fracture continued to make it difficult for me to do this but, as I settled into my new work routine, I also needed to establish a physical fitness training schedule. I needed to be fit enough to pass the Air Force Physical Fitness Test, and to meet the physical rigours of my current role. I had previously passed the running component of the test, but my specialist had strongly advised me that even if I could run, I should not. He stressed that the jarring nature of running would hasten the degradation of my injury, and he reminded me that the crushed intervertebral discs above and below my fracture required my continued care.

I had to become creative in my pursuit of fitness. In Amberley it had been easier to swim than run. There was no shortage of pools and the Queensland climate allowed for it. Swimming in Canberra was not nearly as accessible. I had attempted cycling, but the posture of sitting and leaning forward fatigued my back and increased my pain. So on a warm and sunny Canberra day in February, in a fit of genius, I decided to take up rollerblading.

I had roller-skated as a child and the action seemed to be similar to running without the jarring. Conway's comment of 'I don't think that's a good idea' was already a distant memory as I purchased a pair of rollerblades, minus the protective gear, and headed towards Lake Burley Griffin to give them a whirl. I made it to the first cross street, lost my footing and in a frantic attempt to protect my spine, fell backward on my outstretched left hand. Another lonely stint in a hospital emergency department followed. I sheepishly called Conway to tell him and to hear the inevitable, 'I told you so.'

I fronted up to work the next day with a plaster backslab bandaged to my wrist, while the doctors awaited a radiologist to confirm a fracture. Fortunately for me, there was no fracture and I was able to dispose of the plaster and, albeit in pain, continue with preparations for the Minister's first trip to the Middle East Area of Operations, known in Defence as MEAO. Three months later, when my wrist was still causing me more pain than I felt it should, it was examined under MRI. The MRI confirmed what I had suspected all along: it had been fractured in my fall and, with the activity of the preceding three months, was taking longer than usual to heal. Apparently it would have been difficult to diagnose by plain X-ray.

Confirmation of my fracture and the revelation of my misdiagnosis came long after I had travelled throughout the Middle East assignment carrying body armour and bags. One of my mother's old sayings rung in my ears: 'No brain, no pain.' I thought it was kinder to consider that there were simply no physical limitations to my determination!

Accompanying the Minister to visit ADF personnel serving on operations was the most rewarding aspect of my role as ADC. Of greatest significance at that time was the MEAO. I understood first-hand that the visit of a VIP to an operational area can be an unwanted distraction and possibly even a drain on resources. But I came to appreciate that for the Minister and his staff to be truly aware of the work of Defence and of the value of its members, it was vital they personally witness it at its most extreme. I was immensely proud of what ADF personnel were doing on operations. From the perspective of a Nursing Officer, I gained a much greater appreciation of the individual contributions to Defence capability and the health risks taken by our personnel, whether they were sitting in the middle of the ocean for months on end, being shot at on the battlefield or flying in some of the most challenging environments in the world. I could see that the Minister was equally as proud and at times in awe of those that he had been appointed to serve.

As I observed the Minister's growing admiration and appreciation for Defence members, their work and their families, I began to wonder how I would support him in the event of a fatality. He was a sensitive and compassionate man who, with each passing day grew closer to the men and women of the ADF. Members of the ADF die as a result of illness and trauma, just as other Australian citizens do, and each and every one brings sadness and great loss to the organization and the service of Australia. The fatalities that seemed more extraordinary and at times became complicated were those that attracted media attention.

I observed families who were trying to accept the news of the death of their loved one, also having to plead for privacy, fearful that the media might deny them the opportunity to inform their family and friends in their own way and in their own time. In some cases, there was legitimate concern that the reputation of their loved one might be besmirched by the never-ending news cycle and media speculation about the circumstances that led to the death. Had there been a failure of command, a breach of operating procedures? Was an individual at fault? Seeking the truth that led to death and injury was undeniably necessary but speculation was never helpful. Those in public office know that once a statement or an assertion is made it is forever within the public domain, regardless of whether or not it is true or later retracted if proven not to be true. Defence families of deceased members were thrust into this unwanted spotlight. Unintentionally, such media interest and the necessary investigative Defence procedures have the potential to prolong and complicate the grieving process for military families. Both the Minister and CDF would offer whatever support they could to shield such families, but that in itself was sometimes represented in the media as a 'cover up'.

Nothing sits so heavily on the Minister and the Chief than learning of the death or serious injury of ADF personnel that they have sent overseas. Both Brendan Nelson and Angus Houston dealt with all these Australian families with immense compassion, sincerity and with deep reflection upon their roles.

I was also impressed by how quickly the Minister worked out that it could be difficult to get time alone with members of lower rank. Cheekily, I would often run interference to distract or delay some more senior members to allow the more junior members to have their time. Brendan Nelson was intelligent enough to be able to tell the whining digger from the one with a genuine concern to convey, without the supervision of a senior officer. I fondly recall a trip to RAAF Base Richmond where, upon our departure, we were walking towards the VIP jet and I could sense the relief among the hosting party that the Minister's visit had proceeded without incident. As we approached the aircraft, the Minister made a sharp left-hand turn and headed out across the airfield. Confusion reigned. Where is he going? I knew exactly where he was going.

Beyond the VIP jet, on the other side of the airfield, stood an Air Force Military Working Dog handler and his dog. He had recognized that there was a member of the ADF, obviously working in support of his visit, and there was a dog. The Minister knew to approach military working dogs with caution, but not so much caution as to prevent him from passing on his appreciation to a lone airman who might otherwise be overlooked. Conscious that he had thrown a spanner in the works and, having passed on his thanks, he promptly returned to the aircraft — grinning — and informed all that were waiting that he had just had to say hello to Ron and Spot (names changed to protect the 'guilty') before we left. He would say this in such a way that made it appear they were old friends reuniting briefly, and I am sure that after our departure there were some who would ask the poor dog handler if he had some connection to the Minister of which they needed to be aware.

I was welcomed into the Minister's Sydney home by Dr Nelson and his wife Gillian. Neither would allow me to sit in the car in the driveway if there was any chance that the Minister might be delayed. He bemoaned the fact that their house met all of Gillian's requirements for a family home though not his single requirement that it should include a garage. There was never any cause for me to visit the Minister's Canberra residence, but I had reason to feel that I had some responsibility to his neighbours. One of the more fractious aspects of the relationship between myself as ADC and the Minister was to do with his car alarm. The security system installed in his car, for reasons neither he nor I could understand, was so sensitive and somewhat tricky to operate that it seemed to go off at the most inopportune moments. One such occasion was at a Canberra-based national security agency.

We had driven through the gates to be greeted by a large group from the agency, some of the nations 'senior spooks'. We parked the car and locked it by remote. As we walked away it began to wail at us. Of all the places to demonstrate my ability to maintain security surrounding the Minister, this was not the place to appear lacking. But such was the volatility and unpredictable nature of this alarm. The time and location where the car seemed to demonstrate its needy personality most was in the dead of night, parked right outside the Minister's Canberra apartment. He was intensely irritated by the disturbance it created for his neighbours and, as such, it became an issue for me. I checked the alarm myself and I had it checked by others. I even had it rechecked, until finally, with the appropriate permissions, I had it disabled. I informed the Minister that it had been fixed and that it would no longer cause him any trouble, and it was never spoken of again.

It was not until some years later when I watched *Kitchen Cabinet*, the Australian TV show hosted by political reporter and budding chef Annabel Crabb, that I learned exactly where Minister Nelson had been living during the period in which I was his ADC, and exactly who his 'neighbours' were. He was living in Joe Hockey's shed! According to the show, Joe Hockey, the Member for North Sydney and later Federal Treasurer, shared a Canberra house with Bob Baldwin, the Member for Paterson, and Ross Cameron, the Member for Parramatta. In a shed that had been fitted out as a bedroom, and which Joe Hockey referred to as the 'Summer Palace', lived the Member for Bradfield, Brendan Nelson.

The bright side was that he had his garage, even if it was 300 kilometres from his Sydney home. Again, according to the show, Joe Hockey laughed about 'Defence' turning up in the middle of the night needing a signature from the Minister on an urgent document and being directed out the back to the shed. Who knows what they might have thought, but it is just another indicator of the humility of the man appointed to lead and represent them. As Minister I think that he could have afforded to move out of the shed, but he seemed to enjoy his Canberra residence and the companionship of his neighbours.

I came to know Brendan Nelson as a man who loved his family dearly and who expressed remorse for the family time he had to sacrifice to pursue his career in medicine and later in politics. It was precious time that cost him his first marriage and irreplaceable time with his children.

It was a lesson he took to heart, ensuring that despite his incredibly busy schedule, he would program days in his calendar as 'reserved for family'. He enjoyed playing guitar and took lessons. I was amused to hear that when the then Prime Minister John Howard learned of the Minister's guitar lessons he commented that for a Cabinet Minister to enjoy such a luxury, he obviously mustn't be working hard enough. Anyone who spent long enough talking to the Minister would soon learn that his true loves included the music of Slim Dusty, his motorcycle and, most importantly, his Jack Russell terriers Sniff and Lucy.

I quickly learned to protect the Minister's time as best I could, while still supporting him in his role. Efficiency was certainly paramount and I was even tested by two of my ADF officer friends. Each contacted me and asked me to use my position within the Minister's office to push an issue they felt should be brought to his attention. They each believed that as I was there, they had direct access to the Minister. They did not. I liaised with my contacts within headquarters and worked to have the matters resolved through the appropriate channels and without involving the Minister. Resolution had after all been the intent of the initial phone calls. I never considered that my influence within the Minister's office was that great anyway. He understood how the department worked and had I taken the concerns of my friends to him he would have redirected them through the same channels as I had. There were, however, two significant times when my knowledge and experience were able to contribute to the processing of Ministerial business to achieve outcomes that were to my liking.

The first involved my Defence Health colleagues. During Operation CATALYST, ADF Health personnel were deployed as members of the Australian Medical Detachment — Balad, the same deployment to Iraq I had been denied and which precipitated my departure from ADF Health. Their combined contribution to the coalition health facility was such that they were awarded a Meritorious Unit Citation. Although awarded to the Detachment, which encompassed all three rotations of personnel, it had only been presented to members of the second rotation. The brief regarding the presentation crossed my desk and, recognizing the import of the administrative error, I was upset. I knew personnel in all three rotations. They had been witness to a carnage, the type and scale of which had likely never been seen by Australian healthcare workers. The vast improvements to body armour and casualty evacuation procedures had ensured that combat soldiers were reaching the facility, and others like it, in physical conditions not previously survivable.

I strongly suggested to the Minister that on behalf of the two rotations that had been overlooked and the one that had possibly been embarrassed by being singled out, that he request an explanation. My exact words on his brief were, 'Someone needs some remedial training in attention to detail, regarding matters of such importance'. I knew full well I was sending a rocket in the direction of someone that I was likely to know, but my belief that I barely had a career in Defence Health anymore was easily outweighed by the need to urgently, rather than bureaucratically, remedy the situation. Within two days we received a brief explaining the error and measures to be taken to correct the error. Score one for the ADC!

My second act of influence was much more jovial. It was a requirement of the Minister's role to undertake a great deal of travel, some of which included air travel with No. 34 Squadron, the Air Force squadron that operated the VIP aircraft fleet. On such occasions, involving lengthy flights, I would carry as much paperwork as I believed the Minister would be able to address during the allotted time. Often he would use this time to read briefs or write speeches, but I was always ready with extra work should the opportunity arise. One flight involved the Minister endorsing the proposed promotion of senior officers. The flight had been largely silent, as in his usual manner he worked studiously, poring over his paperwork. Then, he stopped and looked directly at me.

'ADC?'

'Yes, Minister?' I replied.

'The Army is suggesting that I promote Brigadier Anthony Fraser to Major General. What do you think?' I'm not exactly sure why he asked me. It may have been because he recognized that Brigadier Fraser was in Army Aviation as was Conway, or perhaps he just needed a little light relief from his work and thought it amusing to have the Flight Lieutenant's input. Little did he know just how important this Army officer had been in my life.

'Absolutely!' I replied immediately and enthusiastically and went on.

'Following my helicopter crash, Brigadier Tony Fraser was responsible for ensuring that Conway could work in Brisbane while I remained in hospital. Then, twelve months later when I asked Conway to enquire if I could go on a helicopter flight to see how I would react to being on a chopper again, the Brigadier made sure that, when I was fit to fly again, that I had my own Huey and the aircraft captain of my choice. He is absolutely suitable for promotion.'

The Minister smiled, obviously pleased to have a personal connection to the paperwork in front of him. As he wrote upon it he announced, 'endorsed by my ADC, Flight Lieutenant Sharon Cooper', followed by what I recognized as the action of signing his name. It was a story that Major General Fraser later enjoyed hearing from Conway. It provided a personal touch to the General's promotion and hopefully some personal recognition for his wonderful support to us both. Let me be clear, though, I was not responsible for the promotion of Major General Fraser. It was easily a promotion that he deserved and would have certainly occurred without my input.

From the issues that I successfully deflected, to those to which I provided input, there were also those that I was thrilled to witness. My favourite in particular was the purchase and introduction into service of the C-17 Globemaster cargo aircraft. Australia has always suffered from the tyranny of distance and the resulting challenges in being able to adequately project military power and capability. Our ability to move significant amounts of equipment and personnel overseas by air — what's known as strategic airlift — was well served by our fleet of C-130 Hercules, but we needed something bigger.

I had a close connection with the C-130 as it was our primary mode of AME, but when I first saw inside the back of a C-17 I was seduced by its magnitude. All I could see was the potential for greater numbers of patients and greater amounts of medical equipment to be moved across the country and across the world. So it was heartening to hear from the Minister when the decision was being mooted about acquiring the American-made C-17s. His very well-informed response was that it was a 'no brainer', that is to say, acquiring them for use by the Air Force to support ADF operations was something that needed little further thought. Through his prompt acceptance of the recommendation from Air Force, and his strident advocacy within Cabinet, C-17s were acquired in record time and under budget.

From my own professional perspective, the increased payload of the C-17 would be lifesaving in the transport of casualties. Put simply, they could carry more and fly faster and further. They would later prove their worth as Australia's commitment to the war in Afghanistan continued and, little did I know, I would later command a team that would care for and prepare a group of patients for the largest and longest C-17 AME of ADF personnel out of Afghanistan.

In November 2006, we travelled to East Timor to visit Australian Defence Force personnel and to meet with the leadership of the world's newest nation. Of particular interest to me was our scheduled meeting with President Kay Rala Xanana Gusmão, better known as 'Xanana'. His office was located in the Palacio das Cinzas, which translates as 'Palace of the Ashes'. It had suffered damage like many of the buildings in Dili but it had been repaired to a level of function deemed suitable to house the fledgling country's inaugural president. As a man who had engaged in seventeen years of guerrilla warfare in the fight against the Indonesian occupation of East Timor, and a further seven years captive in an Indonesian prison, I expect that he found his presidential office very comfortable by comparison.

As we approached the meeting, I asked the Minister if he would allow me to speak with Xanana. I explained that on the day following my helicopter crash in East Timor, Xanana had travelled to visit me in the UN Military Hospital, but that we never got to meet, as I had already been evacuated back to Australia. He had also sent flowers and a card wishing me to get well, and I wanted to take this opportunity to express my appreciation for his gesture. MINDEF agreed that if there was time at the conclusion of the meeting he would introduce me to the President.

I was permitted entry to the meeting with Xanana and stood quietly at the back of the room, along with many of the entourage. Of all the world leaders that I had met or simply seen over the course of the year, Xanana was one for whom I held a very personal and abiding respect. As I watched him speak with the Minister I recalled the love that the East Timorese held for this man during my deployment in 2000. Posters and stencilled paintings adorned the walls of Dili and the doors of family homes, proclaiming and celebrating his existence with the statement 'Xanana Lives'.

He presented as a quiet and peaceful man, a contrast to the fearless warrior and inspiring commander he had been, as he engaged in a diplomatic struggle with the world. I expect that, like most successful soldiers, he would have probably been more comfortable in the jungle with his comrades than in this room of visiting dignitaries. At the conclusion of their meeting they rose from their seats, shook hands and then with a quick glance to see where I was standing the Minister said to Xanana, 'Before I leave, President Gusmão, I would like to introduce you to my Aide-de-Camp, Flight Lieutenant Sharon Cooper,' and motioned for me to come forward.

As I stepped forward Xanana's gaze remained fixed on the Minister as if he were awaiting further explanation as to why he might wish to meet me. 'Flight Lieutenant Cooper was involved in a helicopter crash here in East Timor, as an aeromedical evacuation nurse in 2004,' the Minister explained.

Xanana's face lit up with recollection and recognition and he looked eagerly toward me. His gaze searched my face, as if he were desperately attempting to recognize me, yet his broad and beaming smile confirmed that he had a memory of me despite having never met me. I extended my hand and bowed my head as he grasped my hand in both of his.

'Thank you, thank you,' he breathed, as he looked me up and down. 'How are you?' he asked eagerly, scanning my body for signs of injury, but there were none to be found. My injuries were well hidden beneath my crisp blue uniform and the facade I had come to master in the preceding two years. But, holding his hand, I felt overwhelmed to be meeting him in person. He was a handsome and charming man and I could appreciate why he was so often described in the Australian media as 'charismatic'. His smiling eyes communicated a greater depth to his life though, a sadness — the struggle, the great loss and responsibility for those who had died under his command, for his cause. The hardship of his 24-year battle to achieve independence in East Timor was not over and I sensed that he carried the burden of the sacrifices made under the leadership for which he was so renowned. I worked up the courage to utter the words that I had been rehearsing in my head.

'President Gusmão, I know that there has been much blood shed in your country and in your struggle for independence.' He nodded. He knew only too well and I did not wish to belittle the enormity of that sacrifice, but nervously I continued, 'I want you to know that I am proud to have also shed blood on the soil of Timor Leste, for Timor Leste, and that I do not regret having done so.'

My words, as sincere as I knew them to be in my heart, sounded unbearably clichéd as they tumbled forth in my nervous and diffident remarks. I felt my cheeks flush. I felt like a silly young girl in the presence of powerful men and yet my words achieved what I had hoped: they spoke directly to Xanana. Perhaps I was being foolish and naive, but I had to find a way to accept my sacrifice, to feel that it had been worthwhile, and now was possibly the only opportunity that I would ever have to truly test that truth.

Xanana drew me forward into a bear hug, squeezing me tight, holding me in his arms, physically reassuring me that he had heard what I needed to say. When he let me free it was simply to hold me at arm's length and to say, 'Thank you, thank you. I remember you.' Then he hugged me once more.

I no longer cared how corny my words might have seemed. I had felt the pain of the people of East Timor and, while there were days when I questioned my choices and pitied my situation, I would never take back the sacrifice that I had made here. To see, to hear, and to feel the deep sincerity of the gratitude of this man, this leader who had served his country in a way that I could not even begin to imagine, helped reassure me that my sacrifice had been worthwhile. It was miniscule in comparison to the sacrifices made by him and by his people and yet, with sincerity, he thanked me for it.

Back in Canberra and as a busy year began to draw to a close, one of the greatest highlights of my term as ADC occurred during my final overseas visit with the Minister. We were visiting Belgium and had spent the day touring the thousands of Australian graves on the battlefields of the Western Front, before we were scheduled to attend the Last Post ceremony at Menin Gate in Ypres. Ypres is a beautiful medieval merchant town, surrounded by walled fortifications and a moat. It was all but destroyed during the First World War but has since been lovingly restored.

As was custom in walled cities, there were gates that led in and out.

Menin Gate was one of four gates leading out of Ypres on the road to the nearby town of Menin. These gates are more like monumental arches designed not just to allow entry and exit but were built to leave visitors in awe. In the reconstruction of the damaged gate, it became a shrine to the tens of thousands of soldiers killed on the battlefield, but whose bodies were never recovered. The churning carnage of the ground war in Belgium and France transformed the land into a quagmire of mud and often a soldier who was injured and fell upon the battlefield disappeared in the mud. Others were so disfigured in death they could no longer be identified. As such, there were thousands who were listed as 'Missing — presumed dead'. It is their names that are carved into the walls of Menin Gate.

Since the end of the First World War, Belgian citizens have held a twilight memorial service with a haunting bugle tribute to commemorate those who died for Belgium. They have done so every evening for almost a century, only ever ceasing temporarily when the country was occupied during the Second World War — the German occupiers having forbade the ceremony. On the occasion of our visit, the Minister would be laying a wreath in honour of Australia's fallen. I had previously visited in 2003 with Conway and was honoured to be back, in uniform, representing the Air Force at such a significant event.

The ceremony was intensely moving. Hearing the haunting notes of the Last Post echo off the walls of the gate, reminded me of Will Longstaff's painting 'Menin Gate at Midnight', which depicts the ghosts of soldiers marching en masse through the gate to the battlefields of the Western Front. I knew the work from the collection of the Australian War Memorial and how it generated incredible public interest on its presentation in the 1920s. Closing my eyes, I could see those ghostly soldiers once more and sense their presence in the still night air. It was a chilling and yet deeply humbling experience. At the conclusion of the ceremony we met with dignitaries and Australian tourists alike. Belgians and Australians brought together in the proud memory of our forebears.

Lost in the significance of the moment, I took some time away by myself. I was still within close range of the Minister but solitary and silent enough to once more read the names of the fallen inscribed upon the walls. The Minister approached me, asking quietly where the names of our Australian soldiers were. I motioned upward to the wall before us and we stood in silent contemplation together. Our year together was drawing to a close and it was moments like this that I treasured; well beyond the corridors of power back home and yet deeply connected to the purpose of our work in serving the men and women of the ADF.

Again the Minister spoke softly, 'That reminds me, Sharon, I think that I have something that belongs to you.' I turned to face him, puzzled and intrigued. What could he possibly have that belonged to me? Had I dropped something? He reached into the pocket of his jacket and produced a set of Squadron Leader rank slides.

'I believe that your Commanding Officer is responsible for promoting you, but as you don't actually have one, I thought that I could step in. Congratulations Squadron Leader Cooper.' I was stunned, speechless. He was grinning from ear to ear and Maria, his Chief of Staff, was busily snapping photos, excited that they could do this for me. It was the most amazing honour to receive my promotion directly from the Minister for Defence amid the memory of the fallen at Menin Gate.

I later learned that the person responsible for the circumstances of my promotion was Conway. He had sent an email to the Minister via one of the Minister's staff, explaining that I had been identified for promotion and that it was customary for the Commanding Officer to promote individuals under his/her command prior to their posting into a position of higher rank. Conway had lovingly detailed my dedication to the welfare of the men and women of the ADF and my passion for commemorating their service. He explained my connection with Longstaff's painting and that he believed that there was no place more fitting for me to receive my promotion than at Menin Gate. He asked the Minister to consider his request and, to my great privilege, he wholeheartedly agreed.

Despite my time as ADC to the Minister, I was never seduced by the political lifestyle. From my brief exposure I learned that the level of responsibility required of a Minister's position, and the number of hours worked, were hardly worth the financial remuneration nor the constant scrutiny of the media and public — those who would often, unfairly, hold our members of office to a standard impossible to be attained by anyone. Of course, there must be standards of conduct that any public servant must respect and uphold, but it should never be forgotten or overlooked that these people are just that — people. As Minister for Defence, Brendan Nelson was as close to understanding what it meant to serve in the military as anyone not in uniform could, and he was passionate in fighting for those who did. He demonstrated that he felt a deep level of responsibility for them and for their families that I had not previously witnessed or have witnessed since. The Coalition lost government in 2007 and therefore so too did Brendan Nelson, a Minister who had made a substantial contribution to Australia's future Defence capability. The disengaging process of strategic reform that would become the hallmark of the ensuing government had a drastic effect on Defence morale.

I had completed my twelve-month sojourn and had decided that political life did not capture my interest enough to stay on. Unfortunately, I still had not had enough time and space to forgive and forget my reasons for leaving my role as a Nursing Officer, or to enable an honest return to Air Force Health. I had gained much personal satisfaction from my work supporting the families of injured and deceased Defence members while with the Minister, and it was time to test the future of my relationship with Conway, so I requested and was granted a posting to the Defence Community Organisation in Townsville.

Many questioned why I did, especially when I could potentially request any reasonably available post with the endorsement of the Minister. I joked that I had asked for a posting to Paris and had been denied. It was time for another relocation, so from Canberra's cold I headed to Queensland's tropical north. But some time before that posting took place, while I was still in Canberra, something of stupefying awfulness occurred.

CHAPTER 9

'HOW DOES THAT FEEL, COPPER?'

May 2006

'Sharon?' enquired the nervous male voice on the other end of the line.

'Yes,' I replied.

'Sharon, your Dad's been shot.'

'What?' This didn't make any sense. My father was a police officer in the Tasmania Police force and had been for almost 30 years. Yes, he carried a weapon for all that time but police officers in Tasmania just don't get shot.

'How do you know?' I said, not believing what I was hearing.

'Look, I'm sorry. I probably shouldn't have called. But I just heard it on the radio and thought you should know.'

'Um, okay. Well thanks. I'll try and find him.' I hung up the phone slowly, still trying to piece together what I had heard and trying to figure out what to do next. I remained seated at my desk, the desk of the ADC to the Minister for Defence. We were working out of the Canberra office for two weeks while Parliament sat. The workaday bustle continued on around me, my colleagues oblivious to the bizarre and disturbing conversation I had just had. I found a phone number for the Tasmania Police Headquarters. I dialled and a woman answered. I identified myself as the daughter of Sergeant Leslie Cooper of the Oatlands Police Station and said to the woman, 'I believe that my father has been shot.' The words just seemed ridiculous. I felt, maybe even hoped, that I was the victim of a cruel prank, but her response was not encouraging.

'I'm sorry, Sharon, but I am going to have to get someone to call you back. What's your best contact number?' Clinging to my knowledge of Defence notification procedures, the process used to notify the family of seriously injured, ill or deceased members of the ADF, I felt reassured that Dad was okay or at least not that bad. In the ADF, such news was never provided over the phone if it were at all possible for the family to be notified in person.

I was in Parliament House, which also housed members of the Australian Federal Police. It would not be difficult therefore to notify me in person through state or federal police channels. Maybe it was a prank after all and the woman who had answered my call thought that she should call Dad and get him to call his delusional daughter. I gave her my mobile phone number and hung up. I thought about calling my sisters and my grandparents, who all lived in Tasmania not far from Dad, but I did not want to upset them if this was in fact just a cruel prank. I would call them when I knew something more.

It was 9 May 2006. The TV news, which continued to drone on in the background, was dominated by the rescue of two miners from the Beaconsfield gold mine in northern Tasmania. They had been trapped a kilometre underground for two weeks after the area of the mine in which they were working collapsed during an earthquake, and this had been the focus of the news cycle now for days. There was no breaking news or tickertape about a Tasmanian police officer having been shot. Surely if it had happened it was newsworthy.

My mobile phone rang. I don't recall who I spoke to, but I think it was the Deputy Commissioner of Tasmania Police as the Commissioner was on leave. He reassured me that Dad was alive and that he was receiving treatment at the Royal Hobart Hospital, after being shot twice in the back and once in the face . . . but he was okay.

'He can't be okay,' I replied. There was silence at the other end of the phone. 'You can't be shot twice in the back and once in the face and be okay,' I insisted. He reassured me again and said that he had seen Dad, had spoken with him and that he was sitting up, conscious and talking in the emergency department.

'Sharon, your father has told me that you are his next of kin', the Deputy Commissioner stated. 'Is that correct?'

'Yes, that is correct,' I replied.

'He asked that I call you and let you know what has happened, as he believes that you will want to come home,' he continued.

'Yes. Of course, I will,' I responded. 'I will just need to book some flights.'

The Deputy Commissioner gave me his contact details and asked if there was anything that I needed. I said I would let him know as soon as I had some flight details. I picked up my mobile phone and walked into the Chief of Staff's office.

'Maria,' I said softly. She looked up from her desk. 'My dad's been shot.' I was still in a state of disbelief as I told her that he was alive and reminded her that he was a police officer. I wasn't sure if that was something that we had ever discussed. 'I'm sorry, but I think I need to go home.'

We walked into the Minister's office and I relayed the news that was now sadly becoming more than just a cruel prank — it was an attack on my father's life. I was pleased that the Minister was there. With his medical background Brendan Nelson would understand that you can't be shot in the back and face and be okay. Those three rounds had all been fired into areas of the body that contained vital organs. Without having to explain my concerns, the Minister immediately understood my clinical perspective. He offered to call his former colleagues at the Royal Hobart Hospital on my behalf.

A perceptive man, he knew that as a military officer and as a Registered Nurse I needed the comfort of a clinical explanation, not the dismissive, 'There, there, everything will be okay.' I left his office to allow him the privacy to make the call. I knew that it was unlikely that Dad's clinical privacy would be betrayed, but the Minister's colleagues were able to reassure him that Dad was okay. That was enough to reassure me for the moment. Now, I just needed to get home. I picked up my things on my desk and headed back to my apartment to pack for Hobart.

Conway was staying with me, having recently returned from his deployment to Iraq as the Army's Official War Artist. He had a week of leave left and offered to come with me to Hobart to see Dad — just one more dramatic event in the life of his girlfriend. Surely, I thought, he was just sticking around out of curiosity for what might happen next. With our bags packed and our flights booked, I raced down the stairs from my apartment with Conway close behind me. My mind was in a whirl. Dad has been shot. He is alive. He is in hospital. He is fine, but he can't talk to me. If he is okay, why can't he talk to me? He has been shot, he is in hospital, he is all right, but he can't talk to me. I shook my head, as if doing so would rearrange my limited knowledge of the event into a more logical conclusion.

'It's okay,' I thought, 'Mum will know what's going on.' I stopped suddenly on the stairs, grasping the handrail to steady myself and bringing Conway to a jolting stop behind me.

'What's wrong?' he asked urgently.

'Nothing,' I replied, shaking my head once more. 'It's nothing.' I knew too well that my mother was dead and that she could not help me. Yet now, in a moment of dire need, she was still my reference point. This was to be the first family crisis without her. I selfishly wished that she were there with him, and at the same time I felt thankful that she had survived her role as the wife of a police officer without ever having to live through this nightmare.

The circumstances surrounding the shooting were trickling in. Dad had been driving south on the Tasmanian Midlands Highway from Oatlands to Hobart. There are only a few highways in Tasmania and the Midlands Highway was well travelled for it traversed the state from south to north — from Hobart on the southeast coast to Launceston in the north. It passed through the sleepy township of Oatlands, an hour north of Hobart, where Dad was stationed as a country cop. He was on a day off, but placed himself on duty so he could deliver a police car to the Hobart police garage for routine maintenance.

He had arranged for his colleague from the Bothwell Police Station, north of Oatlands, to follow ten minutes later to pick him up at the garage and take him back to his station. It was a routine task of no particular interest, but one that had been planned with the efficiency of two seasoned police officers, except for one detail. Dad had decided to secure his service issue pistol at the Oatlands Police Station as it was not necessary for this task.

As Dad drove south through the town of Brighton, 30 kilometres from Hobart, he received a radio call from the Hobart Police Radio Room. They had received a report that there was a vehicle being driven in an erratic manner, heading north on the Midlands Highway. A description of the car was provided. Dad had not seen the vehicle, but had already passed the region in which other concerned motorists had reported the car. Dad radioed his location to the radio room, but they responded that they would contact his colleague from Bothwell, knowing that he was still further north on the highway. Dad told them that he would backtrack and look for the car. He knew that someone could be killed or seriously injured before his colleague found the driver. With both police officers searching, one from the north and one from the south, it was unlikely the vehicle would be missed.

Dad turned north and soon after located the vehicle, which was indeed driving erratically. He was on the outskirts of the quiet hamlet of Pontville when he turned on his lights and siren to attract the driver's attention. He indicated to the driver to pull over to the side of the road. The driver complied. Dad parked the police car in front of the vehicle and notified the radio room of his whereabouts and that he had stopped the vehicle of concern. He got out of his car and approached the vehicle.

Dad noticed that the driver had opened his door and was sitting facing out of the door with both feet on the ground. His first instinct was that the driver was not well, possibly due to alcohol, drugs or perhaps a medical condition. He called out, 'Are you all right, mate?' As he reached the vehicle, he noticed the driver's right arm move and he knew immediately that he was drawing a firearm. Dad had no time to escape and no weapon with which to defend himself.

The driver stood up and faced him, raised his Colt pistol and with no hesitation or warning, fired at point-blank range into my father's face. Dad heard the shot but didn't feel it as it smashed through the right side of his jaw. The bullet bounced off his teeth and took a path around the back of his airway, finally coming to rest against his left carotid artery. Dad stumbled to the back of the gunman's car, knowing that his only defence was to put it between himself and the gunman. He fell to the ground at the back of the car, most likely as a result of sudden and rapid blood loss, and lay face down on the Midlands Highway. It was a stretch of road that he had travelled a countless number of times since his posting as Officer-in-Charge of the Oatlands Police Sub-division.

Now, as his face pressed against the bitumen of the highway, its warmth and roughness against his skin took on a new meaning. He had driven with his young family on this highway over many school breaks as he took us on holidays to the beautiful beachside town of Scamander on Tassie's east coast. He had driven its length, following me on my first big trip on this highway as I left home and moved to Launceston to study nursing at the University of Tasmania — ever watchful of the driving of his inexperienced seventeen-year-old daughter. It was this road upon which he had taken Mum to and from her multitude of surgeries and her chemotherapy and radiotherapy treatments.

I was certain that I had been booked for speeding somewhere nearby to where he laid, on the night that I raced to Hobart to fetch my sisters to let them know that they may only have one more chance to see Mum before she died. It was on this road, also, that my mother's body was taken to the Hobart Crematorium for her final farewell and from where Dad and I would carry her ashes back to rest in Oatlands. Dad could only see the bitumen and the tyres of the car, but he heard the gunman behind him and knew that his only chance of survival now was to play dead — a slim chance, at best. In his head he spoke to Mum, who I'm sure he knew was watching over him, telling her, 'I'm on my way, Louise.'

The gunman saw only the uniform of a Tasmanian Police officer. He stood over him and laughed. He was the incarnation of an evil that can't ever be excused by a pitiful list of poor circumstances or of even poorer choices. He pointed his Colt at my father's back and shot him twice more as he lay defenceless and bleeding on the ground. He then knelt down beside my father, still laughing, and asked, 'How does that feel, copper?'

The gunman was 40 years old. He had a history of escalating violence against police. He had been diagnosed with 'psychiatric disorders' and regularly abused drugs and alcohol. Following a three-day drug binge, he had set out that morning to kill his girlfriend, who lived in the north of the state. My father, who had dedicated his life to protecting others, inadvertently saved her life by getting in his way.

I have always believed that while such dreadful acts reveal the very worst of humanity, they often also prove to reveal the very best. A Registered Nurse on holiday in Tasmania witnessed the shooting as she drove past. Her immediate call to 000 ensured that the response to the incident was as rapid as it could have been.

Two other young men drove past soon after the shooting and stopped after seeing my father lying on the side of the highway. My grandparents later described this unlikely pair as 'rough diamonds', as they had had a chequered past with the police in Tasmania and would possibly have otherwise avoided any unnecessary contact with the law. But their initial thoughts were not of themselves, but of the welfare of my father. They stopped and went to his aid and, realising that he was seriously injured, politely asked his permission to use the police radio! One stayed with him while the other went to the police car and radioed for help, using the best Hollywood-cop jargon, transmitting, 'Officer down!' to whoever was listening on the police frequency.

Then there was Charles Zarafa, who was to receive an award for the bravery of his actions at the scene of my father's shooting. Knowing full well that the gunman was still armed and dangerous, Zarafa confronted him and attempted to engage him in conversation. The gunman raised and pointed his weapon at Zarafa twice before police arrived. According to later reports, Zarafa was so incensed at being threatened by the cowardly gunman that he ripped off his shirt and challenged him to fight. This unorthodox and somewhat foolhardy display of male testosterone was such an effective distraction that when my father's colleague arrived on the scene minutes later he had to pause and wonder which of the two men before him he should arrest first. I guess this is understandable when there are two men facing each other and one is shirtless and acting crazy. Fortunately, the actual protagonist was soon disarmed and lying face down on the Midlands Highway being handcuffed, and a passing doctor was at the scene with the ambulance close behind to assist my dad.

Dad underwent emergency surgery to remove the bullet that was resting alongside his carotid artery. The bullet had grazed and burned the back of his airway, causing it to swell and virtually close, and so he was placed in an induced coma and admitted to ICU until the swelling subsided. I didn't get to talk to him before he went to theatre, and would not get to do so until he regained consciousness. The bullets in his back had lodged in the bone of his vertebrae, stopping them from continuing their destructive path into his chest and abdomen where they may have proven fatal. There was no need for them to be removed, but their presence would result in chronic back pain. The responsibility that I now had, to act upon his behalf without first having had an opportunity to speak with him, weighed heavily on me.

While Australia's media was consumed by the surfacing of the Beaconsfield miners and the lights of the cameras were focused on their politically savvy trade union bosses who took advantage of the spotlight, my father's story barely made page three, yet it still held enough local media interest to warrant a request for a statement from the family. The Tasmania Police public relations officers asked my sisters, me and my dad's parents and brothers and sisters if we would like to make a statement on Dad's behalf. It was the day after the shooting and Dad remained unconscious in ICU. The general feeling among my sisters and my aunts and uncles was that Dad was a private man and he would not want this to be made into a public matter. My grandparents were curious as to what I thought.

My brief time with the Minister had taught me that if we did not provide a statement, then some within the media may seek out other sources of information, less reliable ones, or they might even attempt to make their deadlines by padding the story with details of 'most likely' scenarios. I suggested to my family that it would be best if we controlled Dad's side of the story, ensuring that we were the ones to tell it. They cautiously agreed, placing an enormous amount of trust in me. My grandparents asked me to make the statement.

I fronted a small media conference at Tasmania Police Headquarters, just across the road from the hospital. I sat alone at a long table, facing seated rows of TV and print media journalists and read a statement I had written earlier. I was prepared to confront the likes of the cutthroat Canberra media pack that preyed on politicians, but I soon felt heartened and at home in my quiet state of Tasmania as I was gently questioned by compassionate journalists who respected the work of my father and his colleagues. There was no baying for blood, or any proposal of conspiracy theories, just a genuine interest in the welfare of my father.

While I conveyed the very little we knew of Dad's condition at the time — that he had undergone surgery and was in an induced coma in ICU — and requested that his privacy and that of his family be respected, I recognized that I momentarily had a platform from which to make any statement that I might like. I grasped it to make my feelings known to the media and the world.

'I think that any police officer who puts on the uniform every day understands the risks they take in protecting Australian citizens, and I believe that they do that with pride. I also think that everyone would be saddened that, in my father's case, one of those risks has been realized.' When asked if the dangers of my father's work weighed on my mind, I replied that 'I was proud of what he does for Tasmania and for his country'.

Apparently I handled my first and only media conference rather well. It seemed the police 'brass' breathed a sigh of relief at what they thought was a good interview. When I was thanked by one of the police public relations officers, he asked incredulously, 'Where did you learn to do that?' I pointed to one of his colleagues standing nearby who was grinning from ear to ear, and said, 'He taught me.'

The smiling police PR officer was, in addition to his role as a public relations officer for Tasmania Police, also a member of the Army Reserve and he taught media awareness for ADF members. He had instructed me on an ADF public relations course that was run in Amberley. It was a lighthearted moment at a stressful time that demonstrated just how small the world is and how the lives of like-minded people, in the even smaller world of Tasmania, interact.

What lay at the heart of my statement, and also gave me the strength to withstand the stresses of such an emotional task, was my deep and abiding respect for my father's service and the opportunity that I now had to advocate for the work of police officers and for the support and concern borne by their family and friends. The oath a police officer takes upon joining the Police Force aptly describes it. A newly uniformed cop states that they will, 'faithfully execute the office of police officer in Tasmania, and that to the best of my power, without favour or affection, malice or ill-will, will cause the peace to be kept and preserved and prevent all offences against persons and properties in Tasmania, and that to the best of my ability, skill and knowledge will discharge all the duties of a police officer according to law.'

My advocacy for Tasmania Police was drawn from my passionate desire to stand on behalf of ADF personnel and veterans and the work they do. This passion had begun to develop during my first deployment to East Timor, as it was then that I started to realize the true extent and nature of Defence service. Now as ADC, under the unintended political tutelage of Brendan Nelson, I was learning the power of conveying such incredible and yet too often untold stories, with the emotion that enabled everyday Australians to feel connected to those who served to protect them. It felt good to be able to do this for my father. If only he were awake to tell his story with me.

After a week in ICU, Dad was finally well enough to be brought out of his induced coma and was transferred to a general surgical ward. Another week later he was well enough for me to take him home.

Slowly, his physical wounds began to heal, but sadly his emotional trauma cut far too deeply to be so easily reconciled. Triggered by his brutal near-death experience, but built upon a foundation of 30 years of police service, my father developed post-traumatic stress disorder shortly after his shooting. It was this psychological injury that abruptly ended his police career and plunged him into the depths of grief. A string of losses further complicated his health: he had almost lost his daughter in a helicopter crash in 2004, he lost his wife to cancer in 2005, he lost his job in the bureaucratic nature of the medical termination of his employment in 2006, and would lose his father and then his mother in 2007 and 2012. For someone who had loyally served his community for such an extended period, life had suddenly seemed unbearably cruel.

I left my family in Tasmania once more to return to duty. The gunman was later tried and convicted of two charges of attempted murder and was sentenced to a maximum of fifteen years' imprisonment with a non-parole period of ten years. His sentence has since been increased as a result of other charges relating to his conduct during his imprisonment.

CHAPTER 10

TAKING COMMAND AND AFGHANISTAN

2008

In January 2007, I arrived in Townsville, far from the scene of the horror that had befallen my father and the death of my mother in Tasmania. I could not know that my life would take yet another turn, one that would test me to an extraordinary new limit. I was working as a Military Support Officer at the Townsville office of the Defence Community Organisation. I worked with an Army Military Support Officer providing specific advice to ADF members and their families and military advice to the wider DCO team of Australian Public Service social workers and staff. My duties included bereavement support to the families of deceased ADF personnel, including the arrangement of military funerals and assisting with the Defence aspects of deceased estate administration.

It was a busy job, and one I found deeply rewarding. I was able to continue to work with those bereaved families and ADF personnel I had come to know briefly during my year as ADC to MINDEF. It was the personal experiences of those families, and many others, which had prompted my request to be posted to the Townsville DCO Office.

Towards the end of the first year of my two-year posting I received a request to return to Air Force Health, specifically to No. 1 Expeditionary Health Squadron, Detachment Townsville, providing health support to RAAF Base Townsville. The Officer Commanding Health Services Wing, now Group Captain Tracy Smart, asked to meet with me. She told me the unit was in need of strong and consistent leadership and I was capable of providing it. I was flattered by her personal endorsement and, although I suspected that it was primarily out of convenience as I was already located in Townsville, I gladly accepted the compliment and the posting. But that was not all that was on offer. She presented me with the once-in-a-career opportunity of operational command in a war zone — in Tarin Kot, Afghanistan.

The Air Force was preparing to deploy a Critical Care Team to provide surgical and intensive care capability to the Dutch run, NATO Role 2 Enhanced (R2E) medical facility at Camp Holland in southern Afghanistan. NATO medical facilities are numbered according to the level of care provided. A Role 1 medical facility will usually be situated at a Fire Support Base or Forward Operating Base (FOB) and may consist of a basic medical team. Its job is to receive battlefield casualties and stabilize them before sending them to a higher-grade facility. A Role 2 medical facility will be located at a more established battlefield base and may have surgical teams that include orthopaedics and dental. A Role 2 Enhanced facility will be similar but will include even more medical, dental and/or psychological capability. A Role 3 is a much larger facility and is usually found at a secure base further removed from the battlefield, while a Role 4 facility will normally be back in the home nation. In Afghanistan, most of the FOBs had Role 1 capability.

General Peter Cosgrove AC, MC and Air Marshal Angus Houston AO, AFC were eager to meet with me following my return to duty. Ironically, six weeks after the crash, our schedules aligned and we met at Enoggera Barracks, Brisbane, to farewell the Huey Gunships — helicopters similar to the one in which I had crashed. [Author]

During the evacuation operation from the second Bali bombing (Bali 2), we triaged and prepared dozens of victims. Here, a severely injured Japanese citizen is being prepped for evacuation to Australia for treatment. [Group Captain Bill Griggs; used with permission]

Following Cyclone Larry in Far North Queensland, MINDEF flew into the devastation amidst the continuing stormy weather. It was possibly my worst helicopter flight since my accident, but nonetheless I was never too far behind the Minister to ensure that my ADF colleagues were recognized for their tireless work. [Defence Media Archive]

Meeting world leaders was a definite advantage of the position of ADC. Condoleezza Rice's life and abilities are an inspiration to anyone — especially women — the world over. [Author]

Role 2E, Tarin Kot, Afghanistan. *Left to right:* Me, Flight Lieutenant Heather Dodd, Wing Commander Annette Holian, Corporal Rachelle Kucinskis, Squadron Leader Mary Langcake, Flight Lieutenant Leigh Twist, Corporal Sara O'Rourke, Flight Lieutenant Leslie Lee, Flight Lieutenant Kelli Mitchener, Wing Commander David Scott. [Author]

The Role 2E was surrounded by the ubiquitous blast resistant Hesco walls — a temporary and easily assembled gabion wall which consisted of a wire mesh and heavy duty fabric cage filled with sand and rock. [Author]

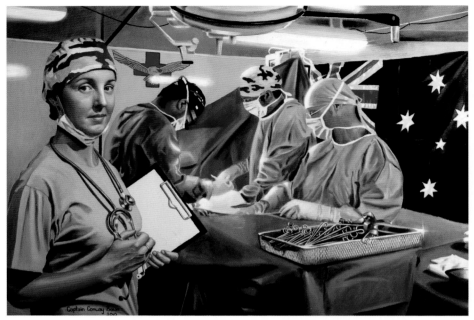

A painting by my husband who was the Official War Artist for the Australian Army, then — after a deployment to Afghanistan as a drone pilot with the Air Force — was appointed the Official War Artist for the RAAF. His portrait of me in the operating theatre as the Officer-in-Charge shows the Australian flag presented to our team by the Australian Special Forces upon our arrival that hung proudly in the OR. [Author]

A candid shot of me during some down time with my team. [Author]

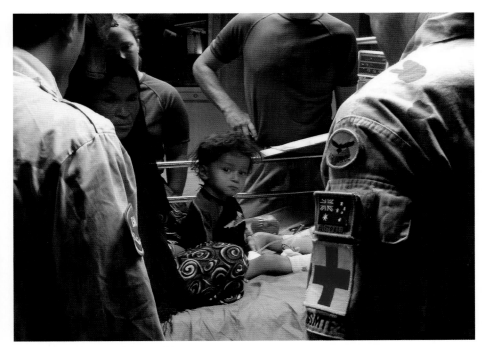

Yet another Afghan child treated by our team. [Squadron Leader Bruce Ashford]

Left to right: Flight Lieutenant Leslie Lee, me, Chief of Air Force, Air Marshal Binskin AM (wearing a theatre hat created by Rachelle's mum), Corporal Rachelle Kucinskis and Wing Commander David Scott. [Author]

View of the Khaz Uruzgan, not far from the village of Ana Kalay. Many of the river valleys had a swathe of green as the local farmers diverted water through trenches and canals to irrigate their fields. [Used with permission by the owner under condition of anonymity]

We sleep safe in our beds because rough men stand ready in the night to visit violence upon those who would do us harm — Orwell

Be an ✶ Aussie ✶ Digger!

After my experiences in Afghanistan, I gained a new respect for the work of the Army and the stereotypical Aussie Digger. This piece of Conway's artwork had a prominent place alongside my desk in Townsville to remind me of what I had seen and for whom I was responsible to provide care. [Author]

Role 2E, Tarin Kot, Afghanistan. *Left to right*: Group Captain Greg Bruce, Flight Lieutenant Leslie Lee, Corporal Rachelle Kucinskis, me, Flight Lieutenant Heather Dodd, Corporal Sara O'Rourke, Wally (Dutch Pashto interpreter), Flight Lieutenant Leigh Twist, Squadron Leader Bruce Ashford, Squadron Leader Sandy Donald. [Author]

At the Australian War Memorial to commemorate Australian service nurses on International Nurses Day, with my career-long mentor and friend Group Captain Michael Paterson DSM, Director of Defence Force Nursing. [Australian War Memorial]

Conway and me, with our sons Austin and Ty. [Author]

Tarin Kot had a Role 2E and Kandahar a Role 3.

The critical care team that I would command would be a ten-member team, consisting of a general surgeon, orthopaedic surgeon, anaesthetist/ intensivist, two perioperative RNs, a perioperative Medical Assistant, two ICU RNs, an Advanced Medical Assistant and myself as a dual-hatted perioperative RN and Commander. Operational command in an area of combat was the ultimate test of my abilities as both a Registered Nurse and a military officer. The opportunity was exceedingly rare and to be considered capable of fulfilling the responsibilities of such a position by Group Captain Smart, a veteran of the 1995 Kibeho massacre in Rwanda, was a tremendous compliment.

In an organization of competitive type-A personalities, my selection for operational command naturally drew the ire of some officers I had considered friends. A year earlier, when I earned what was deemed comparatively early promotion to Squadron Leader, there was a barbed comment among some of my peers: 'It's amazing what a helicopter crash will do for your career.' Now, this new appointment drew the same comment again. I didn't mind, as I considered it to be an indication of just how privileged I was to have been selected. There were also many more who praised my selection and, importantly, those for whom I would be responsible to command expressed the great relief and joy that they had felt on learning that it was me who would lead them.

Six months into my new posting as the Commander of the Health Detachment at RAAF Base Townsville, I bade them farewell and, on 22 July 2008, I deployed to Afghanistan as Officer-in-Charge of the second Australian Medical Task Force (AUSMTF2). We were embedded with and under tactical command of the Dutch, or more precisely the Royal Netherlands Army. In effect we had our own Australian chain-of-command, but day-to-day, the Dutch allocated our tasks. The overall mission was more or less straightforward: provide intensive care and surgical support to the International Security Assistance Force —

Afghanistan, in Tarin Kot, Uruzgan Province. While the medical facility used the official NATO title of Role 2E we came to refer to it more simply as 'the hospital'.

I had been blessed with a highly qualified and experienced clinical team and was to lead them into what was possibly the most confronting and intensely dangerous experience of their lives. The team was divided into two rotations, as the medical team of surgeons and anaesthetists, who were Reservists, had ongoing civilian commitments and were only available for half of the proposed period of the deployment. There was a brief period halfway through the deployment, during the 'Hand Over/ Take Over', where both teams would be present in Tarin Kot. This is not an unusual practice for ADF medical specialists who serve within the Reserve Force.

I had previously deployed with two of the senior specialists within the team and had received positive reports of at least two other members who had previous experience of multiple deployments. So I was confident in their demonstrated conduct under pressure. For the remainder of my team, I felt immensely privileged to be able to share in their journey as they embarked upon their first operational deployment. I knew I would not be able to deliver my team home to their families in the condition in which I had received them.

The burden to protect them from the risks associated with deployment weighed heavily on me. Through the nomination process and through their individual and team preparation for this deployment, they had already changed. They were each reflecting upon their decision to take on such a mission and would be considering if and how they would endure or embrace the challenges that it presented. My goal was to assist them in preferring to concentrate on the personal growth and positive aspects of the adventure that lay before us and, ultimately, on bringing my team home the better for having been there.

I had visited Tarin Kot twice in 2006 with Brendan Nelson but never

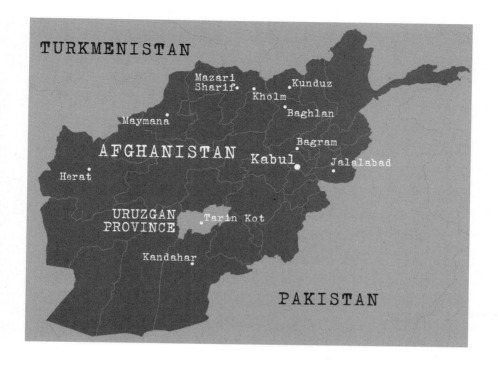

stayed for any longer than a few hours. The security risk was such that the RAAF C-130 Hercules aircraft did not remain on the ground any longer than was needed for them to unload and reload the aircraft, so our schedule was tightly constrained by available aircraft movements. They would drop us off and quickly continue with other flying tasks in the region, before returning to collect us. It had been an unusual feeling to watch your only form of transport leave you behind. The feeling was no different when we arrived in 2008, except that on this trip the C-130 would not return for me for at least three more months.

The stunning beauty of the region remained as it was when I had left it less than two years earlier. Camp Holland was located alongside the township of Tarin Kot, in what was known as the Tarin Kot basin. The township consisted of a collection of modest mud-walled buildings called qallas, set on a sweeping desert plain enclosed by the most magnificent mountain range, with peaks that rose into the heavens, higher than anything I had ever seen before. Their immovable form would provide me with rare moments of solitude within the bustling camp. I would often sit just inside the perimeter of the blast-resistant walls surrounding the camp and look out in wonder at their grandeur. I found that such moments of even the briefest meditation, no matter how challenging my day had been, allowed Mother Nature to remind me of my impermanence in this world. As the likes of our human form traversed the desert floor and played out the struggle for humanity upon its stage, the mountains stood unwavering, watching. Just as they had before we arrived and just as they would long after we had gone.

I often wondered if my future children or grandchildren would return here one day to explore the beauty of these giants in a time of peace. They would land safely in comfort on the airfield below, enjoy the hospitality of the local people and set off to explore the beauty of this land. I would never set foot outside the compound, though, for to do so at this time would mean certain death. My contact with the world beyond the gates would be through the people who, arriving for healthcare, would bring with them the evidence of their lives beyond the walls.

Within Camp Holland, we were allocated accommodation in the Dutch living quarters, directly across from the hospital. It consisted of two rows of armoured shipping containers assembled to face each other and enclosed by a joining roof to create a passageway that could be secured by a door at each end. The passageway allowed for additional living space outside the containers and kept the weather out, which consisted of dust storms in the warmer months and snow in the winter. We did not see snow during our stay, but we saw plenty of the dust of Uruzgan. It was like fine talcum powder that found its way into everything we owned, and when it was whipped up into a storm it could block out the sun, turning day into night and reducing visibility, so much so that aircraft could not land. Running in dust, even on a still day, created small dust clouds around the runner and could bring on an attack of asthma among those prone to the condition.

Inside each of the living containers were two sets of bunk beds positioned along one side and four small bookcases — one for each occupant — along the opposite side. This basic design allowed just enough room between the beds and the bookcases for someone to reach their bed. At least one small bag could be stored underneath the bunks while all other bags, bulky items and boots were stored outside the containers on rack shelving. The most unique and, for some, confronting aspect of our living quarters were the toilets and showers. There was no segregation between men and women.

Each ablution block was also built within a customized shipping container. It consisted of a urinal immediately inside the entry/exit door, and past that, shuffling behind men in midstream, were two single toilet cubicles and the two single shower stalls. I didn't like it but got used to it. So often the working day had been so fatiguing it just didn't matter. The only problem I encountered came one morning after working through the night. I was incredibly tired, and had forgotten to lock the shower door. Halfway through my shower, the door was flung open by a bleary-eyed young Digger looking for his morning wash, only to find me completely naked. I may have made his day or perhaps scarred him for life.

The hospital was also a well-assembled assortment of armoured shipping containers enclosed by an adjoining roofed corridor. The hospital corridor was much roomier than that of the accommodation area, allowing for the movement of hospital beds and equipment. Each container along the corridor acted as a particular medical specialty room, including administration, pharmacy, X-ray, dental, ICU and physio, and each had its own door to allow it to be completely enclosed for privacy and air conditioning or heating. The areas that did not fit neatly into single shipping containers were the general inpatient wards, and the trauma module, which consisted of a two-bay emergency room, two operating theatres, a scrub/X-ray/storage room, and a two-bay recovery room that doubled as an overflow emergency room. These areas were housed in custom-designed armoured containers.

Our hosts and our immediate chain of command, the *420 Hospcie* of the Logistics Support Detachment of the Royal Netherlands Army, welcomed our arrival and assisted us to settle in quickly, so that we might relieve the incumbent Dutch Critical Care Team, and enable them to return home. We had taken part in a mission rehearsal exercise with the Dutch team in The Netherlands as part of our pre-deployment preparation training. Such an experience was invaluable as both teams came to learn that, despite our differences in geographical location, culture and language, our standards and practice of healthcare were very similar. Despite wearing two different uniforms, we very quickly established ourselves as one team. We had forged mutual trust and respect and friendships outside the war zone, and this ensured a smooth transition as we entered the fray in the middle of the Taliban 'fighting season'.

This so-called fighting season, also known as the 'spring offensive', is loosely based around spring and the end of the opium poppy harvest that supplies the bulk of illicit heroin to the western world's drug trade and which funds the war for the Taliban. The weather is 'better' for fighting then, as it is neither too hot nor too cold and therefore allows for greater movement around the countryside. The end of the harvest also frees up manpower to the Taliban. For us, it simply meant an increase in the number of casualties.

I appreciated our supportive relationship with the Dutch. Sadly, my relationship with our Australian Army colleagues at Camp Holland was not what I would call cordial. I relied upon their HQ staff for administrative support to my personnel, including matters such as pay, leave and awards and entitlements. It was made clear to me from the outset by the Australian Army staff that my team was embedded with the Dutch, and therefore it was with the Dutch I should raise my needs.

After nine years in the Air Force, two joint service operational deployments and two joint service postings, I had absolutely no misconception about what my team and I represented to some elements of Army: we were Air Force, and thus carried the 'Blue Orchid' stereotype; we were Health, and thus carried the REMFs or 'Rear Echelon Mother Fuckers' stereotype; and perhaps, most painfully of all for them, we were only deployed on this mission for three months in comparison to their nine months. I understood clearly their perception and it irritated me to realize that their approach to my team overlooked the purpose of our deployment, which was to save their lives if and when it was needed.

Fortunately, our direct Australian operational chain of command was to the ADF HQ in Kabul, and I reported directly to Deputy Commander of Australian Forces in Afghanistan, Brigadier Wayne Bowen, who was very clear about our purpose and our value. Otherwise, we were very ably supported by the Australian Special Forces contingent, who appeared to be very grateful to have Australian 'medics' in Tarin Kot. They had every confidence in the health support provided by the Dutch and the United States, which was of the same standard as ours, but I understood only too well that it was comforting to have health support from those you have previously worked with and who therefore have an understanding of your operations.

They expressed their appreciation with a welcome gift of a full-sized, hand-stitched Australian flag, to be displayed within the hospital. I knew that it was the type used to drape coffins, but in this instance it symbolized the importance of our presence. I was determined that their statement of the confidence they had in our Air Force team would be displayed in the most important way. I presented it to the theatre team and asked them to ensure that it was hung in the operating theatre. It was my wish that if we had an Australian soldier on our table at any time in the ensuing three months, that as they went to sleep and as they woke up, the very last and very first sounds that they would hear would be Australian voices, and the very last and very first thing they would see would be the Australian flag. The team wholeheartedly agreed and the weight of our responsibility in this mission became starkly apparent.

Our mandate was to provide combat health support to the NATO-led International Security Assistance Force — Afghanistan, from July to October 2008. Our Australian team in that time provided the sole intensive care unit and surgery at Camp Holland with a smaller US field surgical team set-up nearby to share critical workloads as needed. Our team was not only mandated to provide health support to ISAF members but also for those serving in the local military and police forces. We were responsible for providing eye, limb and lifesaving surgery to the broader local Afghan population as well.

In addition to providing anaesthetic, surgical and intensive care, the team sought out and adopted additional responsibilities to assist our Dutch colleagues. The surgeons worked within the outpatient clinic and the team as a whole contributed to ongoing clinical education of the combined Dutch–Australian team. The workload was unpredictable and varied in intensity. Some operative procedures took eleven hours and were performed by a single theatre team among a series of other cases. The first patient to be admitted to the intensive care unit was a local police officer who remained in the ICU for 22 days before being transferred to a larger facility, where he eventually made a full recovery.

Flight Lieutenants Leigh Twist and Kelli Mitchener were the only two ICU RNs in the team, so they were each required to work 22 days of alternating twelve-hour shifts. They were ably supported by Corporal Sara O'Rourke, whose rostered hours were often scheduled to cover the period of shift changeover, or split completely to provide assistance within each of the two shifts. Wing Commander David Scott provided medical care and assistance as the Intensivist, otherwise known as a critical care physician, while also continuing to provide anaesthetics within theatre and assistance to the Dutch trauma teams in the emergency department. There was no back-up. For 68 days there was only one team but the team bore no ill feeling about their circumstance. They worked hard, knowing that the mission and periods of high-intensity workload would come to an end. Poignantly, with every patient they cared for, they were reminded of the importance of their presence and of the much greater hardships being endured by others, including their colleagues within the ADF.

The clinical load of each day ebbed and flowed. The local population comprised 68 per cent of our workload, ISAF the remainder. The fact that the local population accounted for more than two-thirds of our workload was not completely attributable to the conflict, but rather to the fact that we were in their country and they were the largest population. They were of all ages and levels of health and fitness and were subject to the risks of their culture and lifestyle. Such risks included poverty, illiteracy, poor access to healthcare, rudimentary transport, ease of access to weaponry and extreme and violent forms of dispute resolution.

If the conflict and the presence of international military forces were to be withdrawn from Afghanistan, all of these contributors to poor health would persist. Sadly, the level of available healthcare would not — a tragic irony of modern warfare. In contrast, the ISAF personnel that passed through the facility were generally young, fit and healthy and had good access to healthcare on the ground and via aeromedical evacuation. Their 'work' practices, although dangerous in nature, were carried out as safely as possible, by a force that was highly trained and well equipped. This was particularly true of the Australian forces. The military casualties rarely presented to us as individuals. They worked in small groups, whether travelling in a vehicle together or on foot patrol together, so if they encountered danger in the form of an improvised explosive device or a battle with the enemy, they did so as a group.

My role was primarily one of command. Working in support of

the CO of the Dutch Role 2E, I was responsible for the provision of intensive care and perioperative services within the facility. At first, I was the primary liaison officer between the team and our Dutch CO, Captain Gemma Flink-Coenen, but as time passed and we began to meld with the larger Dutch team, this became less necessary. My days usually consisted of a morning meeting with the Australian team to discuss matters of administration, security, operational updates and current clinical capability, and an afternoon command meeting with the CO and other clinical OICs to discuss similar issues specifically relevant to the hospital. In between the obligatory meetings and briefings, I assisted as required in the operating theatre and ICU and fulfilled the role of post-anaesthetic care nurse.

As a senior Air Force Nursing Officer my clinical skills were certainly no longer as sharp as those of my Reserve RNs who served in large hospitals in their civilian jobs, so I thoroughly enjoyed avoiding the paperwork to immerse myself in their clinical setting whenever I could. Regardless of my position as their commander, I had no problem in deferring to their more up-to-date clinical instruction and expertise. The perioperative RNs, Flight Lieutenants Leslie Lee and Heather Dodd, were two of the most experienced and resilient perioperative nurses with whom I had worked and I enjoyed stepping into the sanctuary of their operating theatre to observe them at work. Corporal Rachelle Kucinskis held her own as the only permanent Air Force member within the theatre team and rapidly stepped up to the clinical challenge before her, ably supporting a team of officers and keeping the theatre in order. I was able to provide military knowledge and expertise, not otherwise available within the team, and the clinicians provided clinical knowledge and expertise within their field.

Among the steady flow of casualties there were certain days and patients who have remained in my memory more than others. Some had such an impact upon me that at the end of the day I wrote of them in my personal journal. I found that it was a way in which I could critically reflect upon the events of the day before facing the next. The first of our major trauma days provided an interesting cross-section of our patient population. Beginning the day at 0600, we would not see our beds again until 0300 the following morning, with only two, very short sit-down meals for rest in between.

The first casualty of the day was an Afghan National Police highway policeman, who presented with what could only be described as three execution-type gunshot wounds fired at close range to the head, neck and arm. Yet he survived. Those shots should have been deadly but it is possible that, rather than execute him, the gunman had sought to teach him and his colleagues a lesson. One round had been fired across his maxilla, the cheekbone, which is extremely painful but not deadly. Another was fired under his chin at such an angle that it appeared the barrel of the weapon had been used to push his chin upward and his head back. The round that would ultimately lead to his death had fractured the Cervical 5–6 vertebrae in his neck, resulting in paralysis known as tetraplegia — loss of function in all four limbs, with him retaining some function in his arms.

Such an injury may have been survivable in Australia, but in Afghanistan his prognosis was extremely poor. The surgeons debrided — surgically removed foreign matter and any dead or damaged tissue that might lead to infection — closed his wounds and stabilized his fracture with a cervical collar. I later watched the pain and remorse on their faces as they sensitively explained the clinical implications of the injury to the patient — a father of four — and that there was nothing more that could be done. The patient's response was one of annoyance. Not because of the news that he had just received, but because the time that the surgeons were taking in delivering it was interfering with his enjoyment of fresh fruit — a rare delicacy being fed to him by the nurses.

Perhaps he didn't completely understand what he had just been told, perhaps he was simply denying it, or perhaps this was the first clear example that I would witness of an individual of Muslim faith submitting to the will of God — Inshallah: 'If it be God's will.' I had learned that the Islamic faith believes that God has a plan and that if something is written in the plan then it will occur. If it is not, then it will not. I wonder if this belief plays out as a willingness to accept one's fate or a confidence that whatever occurs is as it should be. I reflected upon how lucky I felt to have been born in Australia and I reminded myself that, if I was to ever feel annoyed to be waiting for healthcare in the future, I should remember this man, and his four children who will grow up in this desperate place without him.

The second casualty that day was also a local man with gunshot wounds to the chest and thigh. He was extremely lucky that they were only flesh wounds, and his prognosis was very good, with infection the greatest risk he faced. This man was interesting. He was not keen to talk, or even give us his name, and so he became known as 'the silent one'. It was apparent that our interpreter did not want his identity to be known by this patient and he reinforced the need for us to conceal our name badges when caring for him. I had cause to wonder where the allegiance of this patient lay in this conflict, but as quickly as I did I reminded myself that it was of no importance to me. His existence as a human being and his need for treatment superseded his actions and beliefs when we were called upon to deliver his healthcare.

The final casualty of the day was a NATO soldier who presented with traumatic amputations of both hands. Apparently he was adjusting a grenade on his belt behind his back when it exploded. The ends of his arms were unrecognizable — shredded flesh — yet the remainder of his body was untouched, protected by his body armour. I found myself torn between thinking his luck had been good and yet so bad. One of my surgeons later told me that in his phone call home to his wife he expressed just how lucky he was to be alive, to be able to continue to love her and their baby. His perspective helped me to realign mine. If he felt that he was lucky, then I too felt lucky for having had the honour to meet him, to help him, and most importantly to learn this valuable lesson from him. It would be this reminder of how to choose to frame my experiences in Afghanistan that would assist me in being able to survive them.

At the completion of this soldier's surgery, the anaesthetist, Wing Commander David Scott, inserted fine tubes next to the nerves that supplied his arms, and injected local anaesthetic, which numbed both his arms without making him drowsy. He awoke in some distress believing his arms were gone, but was immensely relieved to find they were there and he was pain free. This technique allowed him to travel home requiring no more than paracetamol for pain relief. This was pioneering use of continuous regional anaesthesia in the battlefield, and significantly contributed to the excellent physical and mental outcome for this soldier.

The soldier was from France, whose surgeons are among the best in the world in the field of surgical prosthetics and hand transplantation. Weeks after this surgery we made enquiries as to his progress and were informed that due largely to the high standard of initial surgical treatment provided to him immediately after his injury, his prognosis for receiving prosthetic hands of good functional capability was excellent. The highest professional praise and appreciation was to be passed on to the surgeon concerned — Wing Commander Annette Holian. She was summoned to parade before the Dutch Commander, so that he might express his thanks personally. In her true unpretentious fashion, she informed the commander that it took a hospital of dedicated staff to achieve such an outcome and that a surgeon does not and cannot work alone.

The greatest clinical lessons to be learned in Tarin Kot were in combat health support. It was what we had been deployed to deliver and yet, aside from orthopaedic surgeon Group Captain Gregor Bruce, who had served in Balad, Iraq, there was nowhere else in the world that I or any members of my team had worked where the rate and complexity of combat trauma was so high. Effectively, we were learning more about combat health support as we delivered it. Personally, I found that despite the tragedy of combat trauma I could preserve my sanity and accept my duty in this war by altering my perspective and accepting that these men had, for whatever reason, taken up arms in this conflict. They were combatants and they had made a choice of sorts, whether good or bad, to be here in this war.

The casualties I struggled to find peace with, and who I continue to struggle with to this day, were the children. I had never dealt with paediatric trauma before and, while the children we saw in Afghanistan were not wounded as a direct result of combat-related activity, they were victims of a society that was at war and that struggled to protect them. Specifically, they existed within a society awash with weaponry. As a much younger Tasmanian nurse during the Port Arthur massacre — one of our country's deadliest mass shootings by a single individual — I embraced Prime Minister John Howard's stringent gun control laws and the greater protection they afforded the citizens of Australia. But it was the children of Afghanistan who reaffirmed for me that the strict gun control legislation adopted in Australia as a result of the Port Arthur tragedy was right. Afghanistan is a country at war, with much larger political issues at hand than tighter gun control laws, but a number of the cases we were involved in demonstrated the devastating impact that results from children living within a society that has free access to firearms, including those that the children themselves own!

Towards the end of our second week in Tarin Kot we were called upon to care for an eight-year-old Afghan boy who had been shot. The domestic shooting was reported to have occurred in the family home in the early hours of the day. The entrance wound and track of the bullet indicated that the boy had probably been innocently curled up asleep in his bed, possibly falling victim to a stray bullet in the house. This was probably not an unusual occurrence in Afghanistan. The facts were never made clear to us, nor were they important, but what was clear was that this young life was in immediate danger.

There was an entrance wound in the back of his left thigh and an exit wound on his back, over his right kidney, indicating that the bullet had passed through his abdomen. On examination, he had several holes in his colon and small bowel. The theatre team worked tirelessly to stem the haemorrhage while I made countless trips to the pharmacy blood fridge, collecting blood transfusions for the young boy as we desperately worked to replace his blood as quickly as it was being lost. Knowing that the boy's older brother was sitting outside the theatre complex, I found myself running to the theatre door, walking calmly past the young man and, once out of his sight again, racing to the blood fridge and back. I lost count of how many times I made this trip, always attempting to prevent alarming the young man waiting patiently to see his brother again. But that never occurred in the way he may have imagined it.

We lost our desperate fight to save this young life. I cannot forget the feeling of that little boy's chest under my hands as I levered my body up and down to pump his heart. Wing Commander Annette Holian, Flight Lieutenant Leslie Lee and I shared the responsibility for CPR, as our colleagues continued to work feverishly to regain control of the haemorrhage, each relieving the other as we fatigued, ensuring that the little boy's body remained oxygenated as we fought to save him. After an hour of pumping and willing his heart to restart, after bringing in a surgeon from the nearby US field surgical team to give us a second opinion, after exploring every conceivable option to save him, as a team we decided that there was nothing more we could do. I watched as the colour drained from his sweet little face. We lost a child. A child who cried for someone or something in his mother tongue as we put him to sleep for surgery. A child who cried to a roomful of strangers who could not understand his pleas. It was my darkest hour in Afghanistan, and possibly one of the darkest hours of my life. How could I adjust my perspective to move on from losing a child?

I would find a way. I needed to at least try to find some light for my team who had fought so valiantly and lost, and who I knew would need to be ready for the next casualty that could arrive at our door at any moment. I found that light in the impact that we had upon the young man waiting outside the operating theatre to see his younger brother again. When he learned of his brother's death, the young man conveyed that he did not understand why we, foreigners, had worked so hard to save a little Afghan boy. We were stunned. My frequent trips to the blood bank had obviously not gone unnoticed. The fact that this Australian team had hunkered down in the theatre for so many hours without a break had not gone unnoticed. The urgent arrival of a US surgeon had also not gone unnoticed.

The translator reassured the young man that, to us, his younger brother was a boy whose life was as precious as any other, and that he was not just an anonymous Afghan boy. The young man was confused and surprised. He was clearly moved that strangers, perhaps even westerners, and women, had done so much for his brother — just an Afghan boy. Unexpectedly, it wasn't so important that we had failed, but that we had tried. Acutely, I did actually feel that we had failed to save this young life, but equally I also felt that we had achieved something great. We had shown a young Afghan man and his family that regardless of race, regardless of religion and politics, there are people in the world who cared for them in their time of need. That is what Australian military doctors, nurses and medics do.

As the team cleaned and restored the theatre, I accompanied the young boy's body to the Recovery Room where the CO had arranged for the Dutch mortuary assistant and the Afghan interpreter to meet and assist with preparation of the body before he could be received by his family. He was delicately wrapped in a crisp white sheet in accordance with Islamic funerary rites, his form appearing even smaller as he lay shrouded upon the bed. There was nothing more I could do for him. I would not watch as he was handed to his brother; there was a limit to my hardiness and my attention needed to turn once more to my team. The CO and I conducted a formal debrief for them, allowing each member to comment on their experience and their feelings. My words felt hollow, but I thanked the team for their work and for their tremendous support of each other.

Two weeks later I was required to enter the operating theatre late at night. The lights were off and, as I only needed to grab a sheet, I decided to leave them off and make my way into the theatre by the light shining in from the Recovery Room. As I stepped into the darkness I sensed that 'the little boy' was there with me. I felt him wanting to get my attention, to let me know that he was there. I'm not sure that I believe in ghosts, but my mind made it quite apparent that I had a very strong memory of a significant event associated with that room. In the absence of the usual daily mass of sensory stimulation in this busy operating theatre, including the light, it was this memory that made its way to the forefront of my mind.

I wondered if perhaps I needed to find some time, somewhere, somehow, to process a few more of the events of my days in Tarin Kot, before those memories came back to me unexpectedly on their own at a time and place that was not appropriate. It was a poignant reminder of self-care early in the deployment. At the time this occurred, I was not a mother but now, years later as I write this and as the mother of two beautiful boys, the memory still brings me to tears. I feel his chest beneath my hands and I will never forget that sweet little face.

About one-third of our surgical work involved children. I cannot recall precisely but of 81 casualties about 27 were children, and of those children only three were girls. With a guesstimate of the population being roughly 50–50 girls and boys, we should have seen 13 girls or, then again, maybe the same number of girls as boys, about 27 each. But we saw only three. One girl, a teenager, was brought in by her father with persistent abdominal pain. In a culture where young women of child-bearing age were sequestered away, her presence in our western male-dominated military camp was unusual. She appeared delicate and docile yet we could not have imagined the level of physical and emotional resilience that she would display.

She required surgery for suspected appendicitis, possibly peritonitis. Despite the agonizing pain that we expected she was suffering, she and her father had walked for two days to reach us. Prior to surgery she had hopped on and off the hospital bed three times — the first to be examined, the second after being weighed, and the third to climb onto the operating table. So severe was her peritonitis that the surgeon drained two litres of the most putrid-smelling pus from her abdomen. Not once since we met this girl did she complain and nor did she throughout her post-operative stay. We were stunned by this girl and by her father, who had entrusted his daughter to the care that saved her life. I felt encouraged that in a culture where women were considered subordinate to men, the love of a father for his daughter had prevailed. But maybe I was just being naive.

Such a glimmer of hope was to be challenged by the stark reality of life in Afghanistan for a three-year-old girl brought to us by her grandmother. She presented with third-degree burns to her feet that were so extensive that she was missing skin, toes and enough flesh to reveal her tiny bones. It was impossible looking at the injuries to not know she would forever bear such horrendous disabling scars. It seemed implausible that anyone would stand in a fire long enough for such hideous damage without recoiling from the pain. Our interpreter shared our doubts. A more likely explanation was the common form of discipline for children in Afghanistan that involved holding a 'naughty child's' feet over a fire.

I was sickened and hoped this interpreter was wrong. My resilience to the realities of the world was being tested. Afghanistan was revealing the evil that humans can do to each other, whether it be the deliberate placement of improvised explosive devices that were so indiscriminate in their wounding and killing, or this type of barbaric and life-lasting punishment of a child not yet old enough to understand the reason for her punishment. How could an adult feel no empathy for the child? As the sun set on another challenging day I turned to the solace of my journal:

Our children do not choose to come into this world. They are invited. An adult, or at least a person of childbearing age, chooses to extend that invitation. Sadly, sometimes that choice is made with little thought for the consequences, sometimes that choice is made without the consent of the other adult and sometimes it is a choice made of violence when a child is conceived from rape. Our children are the true innocents of our societies. Until they have the maturity or the legal ability to protect and defend themselves they rely on us, the adults, to do that for them. In far too many cases we fail. In an age where technological advances have allowed us to hold the world in the palm of our hand, children die from preventable neglect, choking on intestinal worms in East Timor or gunshot wounds in Afghanistan. It is a shame that humanity cannot be programmed like the latest and greatest smart device, or traded on the share market to profit the world's wealthiest one per cent. Perhaps if it could we would invest in it more and work harder to protect it.

I was curious as to why this child's grandmother was permitted to bring her into our camp unchaperoned by a male. The interpreter explained that as she was no longer of child-bearing age she was now considered nearly equal to a man and didn't require the protection of the men in her family. I pushed for more information as to why we were not seeing more Afghan women. He explained that it was not an indication of a lack of care of Afghan men for 'their' women but that the security measures at our camp prohibited them from entering. All visitors were required to pass through military checkpoints that involved a pat down to ensure the visitor was not armed nor had a suicide vest or device strapped to their body. While this physical contact was absolutely necessary for our protection it was unacceptable for Afghan women or girls to be touched in such a way by a western man, or indeed any man other than her husband.

I tried to remain open-minded about the treatment of women in Afghanistan and I thanked the interpreter who told me it was his great hope that his sisters would go to school even though his father refused to allow it. I wondered what Afghan men thought of western women within the hospital and more importantly what young girls thought of us. The Dutch and Australian commanders, the two Australian surgeons and two of the Dutch General Practitioners within the hospital were all women. Was it their perception that we did not know our place? That western men were somehow weak for allowing us to become educated and 'powerful'? Or did we give them a glimpse of the great potential of a society that strives to value the equity and diversity of its people?

It was not unusual when working in the hospital for us to remove our overshirts and work in our brown T-shirts. It was cooler and also a more practical form of clinical dress. It became very apparent that such attire, although loose, was fitted enough to reveal the shape of our breasts, something made apparent to us from the very obvious stares of the Afghan men. There was no doubt that this was something they had not seen before. It made us uncomfortable, just as it would in Australia, but there was no experience of explicitly inappropriate behaviour. We simply resolved to wear very baggy shirts when caring for our Afghan patients.

Working as a combined Dutch–Australian team, there was an unspoken disquiet about receiving casualties from the Dutch and Australian forces. The first casualties were Dutch. A patrol had driven over an improvised explosive device, injuring all on board. There were no fatalities, but of the four injured there was one young soldier who undoubtedly survived only because of the combat first aid that he received in the field. He received multiple injuries, but his life was threatened by the one injury that literally tore him apart. His perineum — the area between his scrotum and his anus — had been ripped open by the blast, with his wound extending down the inside of both legs. His blood loss was so great that we came close to exhausting the available blood supply on his treatment alone. The theatre team worked for eleven hours to stabilize him for immediate aeromedical evacuation out of Tarin Kot, before proceeding with surgery for one of his colleagues.

The Dutch Army health units worked closely with their deployed forces and knew many of their own soldiers as friends. They were visibly shaken by the incident and the ensuing casualties. Once they had provided the necessary resuscitation and triage, they were then faced with their first challenge of trust in us when they handed them over to us for the next, and more intensive part, of treatment. We understood this. While Australians were to provide the critical care capability required to treat this young Dutch soldier, it was not difficult for us to ensure that the Dutch were involved in every aspect of his care or include Dutch Medical Officers in the operating theatre during every one of those eleven hours. Yet, in the days that followed, our team was the one to receive the multitude of accolades for this effort to save the life of a Dutch soldier. The Dutch Commander was impressed with our stamina. He remarked that he would 'have us in his battlegroup any day'.

The gratitude of the Dutch and of ISAF was inspiring, but the AUSMTF2 medical team acknowledged that the soldier's life was actually saved by some anonymous soldier/medic on the battlefield who had had the clinical foresight and courage to pack his wound with two

Quikclot Combat Gauze dressings — a gauze pad impregnated with a haemostatic compound to promote blood clotting and stop bleeding. It was this action that slowed the life-threatening haemorrhage and ensured the soldier would survive long enough to reach surgery.

I discussed this with the CO and, after making some enquiries, she discovered a Dutch nurse and a combat medic in the field had treated the soldier. Apparently, as the nurse went through the assessment and resuscitation of the casualty he instructed the combat medic — who was all of eighteen years old — to pack the wound with Quikclot. Considering the age of the combat medic, the horrendous and confronting nature of the soldier's wound and the terrifying circumstances in which the treatment was required, I suggested to the surgeons, Wing Commander Annette Holian and Squadron Leader Mary Langcake, that they put their opinions on paper and recommend the nurse and the medic be commended for their actions. They did so and some weeks later the pair received awards for their quick thinking in saving the life of their comrade on the battlefield.

Just two days after treating the Dutch casualties we received our first Australians. It was to be a long and drawn-out night of waiting for us, but it would be nothing compared to what our Australian colleagues were enduring in the field. I had not long been in bed when at 0100 I was awoken with the news that there were Australian casualties inbound. I got up, dressed and headed over to the hospital for a briefing. I felt my adrenaline surge as my anticipation of what lay ahead began to build. An Australian patrol had hit an improvised explosive device and a number of casualties were on their way to us in a US Black Hawk 'Dustoff' helicopter.

The Dutch readied the emergency room to receive the casualties and I notified the theatre team that we may have some work to do but there was no need to get too excited until I had some more details. Then we sat and waited. I hated the waiting. We were ready yet we waited. The next briefing we received was even more concerning than the first. We were told to stand-down. The AME Dustoff helicopter had made a 'hard landing' — that is to say it crashed and was damaged — at the site of the casualties and there would be no further attempt at retrieval until sunrise. The casualties were being treated at the scene and were stable enough to wait until first light for another attempt at AME.

We were supposed to go back to sleep and await further instruction in the morning. I knew what it was like to wait as a casualty at a crash site, but I had only waited for a short period and was surrounded by concerned locals. I had not been waiting in the middle of a war zone surrounded by enemy whose sole aim was to kill me. I broke the news to my team, who were as concerned as I was, but I still relayed the same ridiculous expectation to them that had just been relayed to me — I needed them to go to bed and get some rest so that we were prepared for whatever the morning might bring.

As I wandered back to the accommodation block I looked up at the night sky, knowing that somewhere out there a group of injured Australian soldiers was probably looking at the same scene. They were likely to be only tens of kilometres away and yet their being on the other side of our defences made their situation far more perilous than mine was ever likely to be. I hoped that wherever they were, that they could hold on.

We were all up early, anxious to learn of the situation. There was little more to know until we received a Nine Liner, a format of communication that provide nine lines of details about the casualties. This one told us their AME was on its way to our location and the status of the patients inbound. When they finally did arrive we sprang into action to triage and treat the wounded. There was no need to open the operating theatre and I was assigned to monitor one of the young Special Forces soldiers awaiting the results of some X-rays. I had never known a patient so eager to escape a hospital bed. He was a wiry red-head in desperate need of a wash. I wasn't aware of how long they had been in the field and I wasn't likely to be told, but they were all filthy. They had, of course, just survived a blast, a helicopter crash — either inside or outside the chopper — and a night standing-to, awaiting an enemy attack.

My patient had some suspected fractures along with a few cuts and scratches but he was hell-bent on convincing everyone around him that he was okay and there was no need for him to be there. As much as I wanted to give him permission to relax and to feel safe, he didn't want a bar of it. He just wanted out! I couldn't tell whether he was still riding the adrenaline high of the incident or the fear of an imminent decision that might send him back home. A senior soldier from their unit arrived to check on them, spotted my cagey patient and began congratulating him as he approached from across the room. Apparently, while this soldier was blown several metres from his vehicle with the force of the blast, he never let go of his 'gat' — a colloquial term derived from 'Gatling gun', which soldiers use to refer to their guns. The recollection stirred the other soldiers to add their version of the story to the mix, and for the soldier in my care to humbly own up to the remarkable feat.

I was stunned. In my recent experience of choosing the perspective of a situation that best enables you to carry on with the job at hand, this was my favourite. This young man had just survived a terrible life-threatening ordeal, not once but at least twice in a very short period of time. Rather than dwell upon the dangers confronted or the tragic possibilities that were avoided, they rejoiced in the feat of strength that may live on in a legend that others might strive to exceed. With no fractures, a relieved and eager soldier left my sight as quickly as he could, promising to follow the doctor's orders to rest. I had my doubts that he would, but I felt relieved that they were all safe and that I had played some small part in closing that exciting chapter of their deployment.

A little over two weeks into the deployment, we had well and truly established ourselves within the Dutch team. We were presented with their deployment T-shirts and hats as a true military-style seal of our now being one of them. I had often said to the members of AUSMTF2 that our mission was as much about diplomacy as it was about combat health support. We were embedded within the capability of another nation and we needed to ensure that we respected that privilege while sharing and remaining true to the customs and traditions of our own service. It was an aspect of my role that I took very seriously and one I believed I had achieved when Captain Flink-Coenen appointed me with the responsibility of the hospital's Duty Officer. It was a role that had previously been shared between herself as the CO, and the Senior Nursing Officer on an alternating 24-hour roster.

The Duty Officer managed the hospital on behalf of the CO. This included facilitating incoming casualty reception, treatment, accommodation and transfer in accordance with the current bed state and the available clinical capability, all of which was then to be reported through the ISAF chain of command at the conclusion of each day. Such a responsibility added to my daily workload, but it also demonstrated that I had earned the respect of my Dutch colleagues and had found some value among them that was greater than simply being a liaison for the Australian team. To my knowledge, I was the only Australian to have ever been afforded such a privilege.

The cultural challenges of providing healthcare within a country other than your own can have a drastic impact upon the approach needed to achieve the best possible clinical outcome. While the living conditions of the people of Afghanistan had a significantly adverse effect upon their health, I had not truly considered the impact that would result from their faith in Islam. Nor had I ever imagined that in the middle of dealing with such a challenge, I would also be hosting a VIP visit.

We had been notified that we would be receiving Chief of Air Force (CAF) Air Marshal Binskin AM, affectionately referred to by most Air

Force personnel as 'Binny'. It seemed that I was the highest-ranking Permanent Air Force Officer currently serving at Tarin Kot, or at least the one deemed to be most appropriate to host the Chief during his visit. I had on two previous occasions been a member of a visiting VIP party in Tarin Kot when I was ADC to the Minister for Defence, so I guess it was fair that I now experience the disruption of such a visit from the other side.

I briefed the team and the CO on the timings and arrangements of the visit and my plan for him to visit both the ICU and the operating theatre teams in their work area. The ICU team was still caring for their first patient, who was now conscious, and they were therefore always on-duty, so there was no choice but for the Chief to visit them in their place of work. I joked that the remainder of the team would probably be in the operating theatre, also in their place of work, by the time I arrived with the Chief.

As I readied myself to travel to the airfield we were notified of a casualty at the gate of the compound. He was a fourteen-year-old boy with a gunshot wound to his left leg. It certainly sounded like a reason to open the theatre, so I delayed my departure for as long as I could so that I could assess the proposed course of action and adjust the Chief's visit as required. The young boy had been sitting with his shotgun — yes, his own personal shotgun — resting in his lap, when he decided to pull the trigger. I didn't see that there was any need to ask why he would choose to do that. He was a fourteen-year-old boy. Grown men do stupid things just to see what might happen. But why does a fourteen-year-old boy own a shotgun? Because he lives in Afghanistan! Sadly, he now had a gaping wound where his left knee should have been.

The timeframe between injury and presentation to the hospital was uncertain, but I knew that the surgeons would have to decide whether they could repair or whether they must amputate the limb of a young boy. I also knew that they were quite capable of doing so without my presence, so I apologized for having to go and told them that I would return with the Chief.

I greeted the Chief and his party at the ramp of the RAAF C-130 that had delivered him to Tarin Kot. We climbed into the back of a Bushmaster PMV — an armoured protective mobility vehicle — and headed towards the hospital as I explained to him who I was and why I was in Tarin Kot. I went on to explain the role of AUSMTF2 and that, at present, every single member of the team was occupied in their deployed role, but that they were keen to meet him if he was comfortable to enter their area of work. He listened intently to everything that I said, or maybe it was so loud in the back of the Bushmaster that he had to lean in just to hear me. Regardless, he was keen to meet the team and agreed to do so on their turf. I was a little apprehensive about what I was about to do to the most senior person in the Air Force . . . my boss!

The visit to ICU was straightforward. The patient, our first in intensive care, was a local police officer, conscious and alert, so he wasn't as confronting to see as a sedated and intubated ICU patient might be. I was impressed by the Chief's approach to the patient. Having greeted the team, he asked them if he could meet the patient and, with the assistance of the interpreter, they were introduced. The Chief extended his hand and the patient took it in both of his, visibly moved by the presence of his unexpected visitor. I didn't know Air Marshal Binskin, but the measure of the man was evident in that momentary interaction. For years I had witnessed professionals walk in and out of hospital rooms without a glance at the patients within them. I had seen doctors and nurses review a patient's chart at the end of their bed without any interaction with the patient. The Chief had no obligation to the patient in this room, but it was clear that he respected the work of the Air Force team before him and the human being for whom they were so tirelessly providing care. Yet this interaction would be surpassed in meeting the theatre team.

We left the ICU and headed toward the operating theatre. As we walked, I began to provide the Chief with a brief explanation of the patient currently inside. I also explained again that six of the ten members of AUSMTF2 were in the operating theatre and would not be able to leave their patient to meet with him. If he wanted to meet with them he would need to enter the theatre. We established that he had not visited an operating theatre before during an ongoing case and so I explained that, regardless of the state of the patient, he might find that the environment would make him feel faint. I explained that the lights, the smells and the very closed quarters often had that effect on people, so I would keep him near the door so that he could leave at any time he chose to or we could drag him out if he was physically unable to. He remained keen and I began to wonder how much trouble I was about to encounter if he passed out.

As we reached the door, I asked him to cover his boots with paper covers and his hair with a hat. I had set aside an AUSMTF2 custom theatre cap that had been made by Corporal Kucinskis's mother and which Rachelle wanted to gift to the Chief. As he stood with his back to the theatre door and with me facing him ready to take him to the team, he grinned and said, 'Sorry, Sharon, I don't like hats.' I wasn't sure if he was joking and I didn't really have time to decide. All I knew was that a theatre cap was a condition of entry and that he would not be judged kindly by the staff if he walked in without one. He had a neat military haircut and he wasn't about to shed hair onto the surgical site, but I chose to stand my ground.

'Sorry, Sir, but you can't go in without one.' Still smiling, he took the hat and put it on and I will never know whether he was joking, testing me, or being honest about a dislike of hats.

The team was impressed and proud to have him there, and greeted him as best they could while continuing with their work. Squadron Leader Langcake momentarily stepped back from the fourteen-year-old

Afghan boy on the table to provide a brief clinical explanation while I kept my eyes on the Chief. He was as cool as a cucumber, as able to engage with the team in this environment as in any other. He thanked the team for their efforts and for allowing him to visit them and we left them to their work. Pausing for a cheeky photo opportunity with the Chief in his hat, I thanked him for what he had just done. It was then that he confided that he had a son the same age as the boy on our table. My heart sunk as I realized just how much my idealistic plan may have confronted him and I thanked him once more.

The remainder of his visit to Camp Holland and to the non-health Air Force elements was far less dramatic and after two hours on the ground I accompanied him back to the waiting C-130, shook his hand and wished him a safe trip home. As anyone who has been on operations knows, to have saluted him on an open airfield in the middle of Tarin Kot, not knowing what enemy elements might be observing, would have not only been tactically unsound but also the ultimate insult.

Back at the hospital, the theatre worked on. The young Afghan boy was transferred to ICU for observation overnight but, as I retired to bed, I had little doubt that despite the best efforts of the surgeon his foot was dead. I knew that the next day would be another challenging one, for none more so than a young boy who would almost certainly have to face up to the amputation of his leg.

The clinical workload of the following day began with Wing Commander Holian meeting with the father of the young boy in ICU to discuss the need to amputate his son's leg in order to save his life. I stood patiently outside the room in which they were talking. My duties were dual that day, as I needed to know the theatre timing as the Duty Officer responsible for co-ordinating other treatments, but also as the Australian OIC. She exited the meeting room and walked toward me in a somewhat harried fashion and reached out to grab my arm. The father was walking away from us towards the ICU.

'The father would prefer that his son die with his leg than live without it.' Her statement was as clear as it was shocking.

'Jesus Christ!' came my response. It probably was not the most appropriate phrase to be using in relation to a clinical case complicated by the Islamic faith, but the words escaped me in pure instinctive reaction to the shocking statement.

'It's all right,' she reassured me. 'We saw this in Banda.' I loved the confidence and optimism of her years of both clinical and military experience. I was still reeling from the news that a father would prefer his son died with his leg than live without it and Wing Commander Holian was already moving onto the next feasible option. She explained to me that it is the Islamic belief that in order to go to heaven one's body must be whole, therefore if we amputated a part of his body we would be condemning him to an eternity of exclusion from paradise in the afterlife. The father was choosing his son's eternal place in heaven over his comparably shorter existence as a mortal here on earth. It made sense if you believed in it. Both Wing Commander Holian and Group Captain Scott had previously encountered this when they deployed to Banda Aceh in Indonesia following the Boxing Day Tsunami in 2004, where the population was of the Islamic faith and had suffered death, destruction and all manner of trauma, often requiring the amputation of limbs. The method used by the medical teams there was about to be proposed here.

We followed the father down the hall toward the ICU where he intended to inform his son of his decision. Wing Commander Holian followed, accompanied by the Afghan interpreter, and once again that morning I stood outside and awaited an answer. The father reinforced his view to his son and denied him the required amputation to survive his injury. He was convinced that there was treatment available in Pakistan that could save his son's leg and refused to believe Wing Commander Holian's assertion that that simply was not true. She offered the 'Banda

Aceh solution', which was to provide the boy and his family with his amputated leg, so that it could be buried in the boy's future grave. As long as the boy was buried in the same grave as his leg when he died, hopefully much later in life, he would still be whole. The father did not accept this. The ICU team began to prepare the boy for discharge, knowing full well that if he left the hospital at this stage he would die of gangrene that would develop in his now necrotic left leg. I readied myself to support them, not knowing how on earth I would begin to achieve that.

Left alone to consider the conversations he had just witnessed, the young boy became defiant and insisted he did not want to leave the hospital and he certainly did not want to die. Then, surprisingly, with the very skilful and assertive language skills of the interpreter, the boy and the interpreter convinced the father that there was merit to Wing Commander Holian's proposed solution. Surgery was scheduled and, although it is never easy to concede the amputation of a limb, the young boy's life was saved. I cherished the contribution of my specialists that day more than any other. In respecting the beliefs of another that day, we would have also had to respect the needless death of a child. Carrying his leg from the operating theatre to the mortuary and then witnessing it being handed to the boy's family was sad enough. But then, that is the egotistical view of an infidel — me.

The following weeks and days would have us unknowingly prepare the hospital and ourselves for the aftermath of an historic Australian battle. The ICU patient for whom we had been caring for 22 days was transferred to the medical facility at Kandahar, allowing the ICU team some well-deserved respite. They had worked so hard for so long that to see them outside the ICU and their living accommodation was akin to welcoming the arrival of three new team members. Shortly after, that would actually be true, as we reached the midway mark of our deployment and we welcomed the arrival of our second rotation of specialists.

Group Captain Gregor Bruce, Squadron Leader Sandy Donald and Squadron Leader Bruce Ashford arrived like a much-needed breath of fresh Australian air and brought their own brand of humour at a time when the team needed it most. Whether they realized it or not they did not carry the burdens of the deployment thus far and so lifted the spirits of the team. Group Captain Bruce, a mad keen runner, would ask me daily if I would let him go for a run beyond the wire! Squadron Leader Ashford was always there when I needed him, chilled out with a Dr Pepper in hand, and Squadron Leader Donald, a modest 2 metres tall felt at home among the equally tall Dutch who went to 'great lengths' to build a bed in which he could sleep comfortably.

Due to some poor logistical co-ordination that was no fault of the incoming team, AUSMTF2 unexpectedly had its full complement of thirteen personnel for seven days. But this poor co-ordination ended up being a blessing, for we had the maximum number of personnel available to deal with the casualties of what would become known as the Battle of Ana Kalay, also known as the Battle of Khaz Uruzgan. Although I was never aware of the intricate detail of the combat operations occurring outside the wire, this battle will be one that will always remain with me.

The day began just like any other, but it would end with an operating theatre full of Australian casualties who, along with their American comrades, had fought their way out of a battle where they were outnumbered five to one. I would later learn that in the preceding days, a troop of Australian SAS Special Forces soldiers had set out to capture a senior Taliban leader. Upon arriving at their destination at US Firebase Anaconda in the Khaz Uruzgan district of Uruzgan Province, about 70 kilometres northeast of Tarin Kot, they received intelligence that the intended target was now no longer in the area and that their mission had been cancelled. With no immediate task at hand and their return transport still days away, they offered their time and services to their American colleagues. The Americans were appreciative of this and informed them that there were two valleys nearby that they would like to try and enter in order to engage the enemy. It has been reported that the stereotypical Aussie response was something along the lines of, 'Yeah . . . we'll give it a go!' Why take advantage of a few days' rest when there was work to be done?

The Australian SAS sniper teams were to enter the valley by foot under the cover of darkness and set-up firing positions on the high ground overlooking the valley floor. The Americans, with their Afghan interpreters, were to enter the valley in their armoured Humvees, making no attempt to conceal themselves but to intentionally draw the attention of the Taliban fighters. When the enemy rushed to ambush the American convoy they would be met by the accurate and deadly fire of the Australian snipers above.

The first engagement of the coalition tactic was successful, with eleven Taliban fighters confirmed dead. The SAS sniper teams stayed in the valley overnight while the Humvees headed back to Firebase Anaconda with the intention of repeating the tactic 24 hours later. However, events were to play out differently the next day.

The Australian snipers had moved positions into the second valley of interest, near the village of Ana Kalay, and awaited the arrival of the American Humvees, which were joined by a dozen more Australian SAS, two Australian engineers and an Explosives Detection 'sniffer' dog. Before the vehicles entered the valley, the Australians with the convoy dismounted and climbed to higher ground to adopt their own ambush positions. The sniper teams were elsewhere on the high ground already in their positions from the night before. The tactic proved successful once more, with a number of Taliban fighters killed in the ambush. It would be the coalition troops' decision to withdraw from the valley later that day that would run into trouble.

The Australian sniper teams decamped their positions and headed back to Firebase Anaconda on foot over the mountains, while the remaining

SAS positioned in the higher ground returned to the convoy of Humvees for the drive back to base. So narrow was the valley that they had no choice but to return the same way they had come — a decision they knew was not ideal. It would then have become rapidly even more concerning when they heard intercepted Taliban radio transmissions calling for their immediate slaughter, with the words, 'Kill them! Kill them all!'

Amid a hail of mortar shells, rocket-propelled grenades and small arms fire, the coalition force was vastly outnumbered by over 200 enemy insurgents. Much has been written about the Battle of Ana Kalay and the ensuing feats of survival and acts of valour that saw the group of Australian and American soldiers successfully withdraw from the valley, heavily wounded, but with just one fatality, an American soldier. However, little has been written about the medical response to the multiple casualties.

I was the hospital's Duty Officer that day when the Nine Liners began to roll in. I began to wonder where the final number of casualties would end. It was immediately apparent that we were about to receive the largest group of casualties at one time in our deployment so far. The CO immediately instigated the Mass Casualty Plan and all available personnel reported for duty. Based upon the numbers and nationalities of the casualties, we knew that the American Forward Surgical Team (FST) located nearby would be preparing for a similar influx of patients.

Wing Commander Holian, in the role of Clinical Director, was solely responsible for the triage of incoming casualties. She met each one at the receiving area immediately outside of the emergency room, conducted an assessment of the soldier's condition and assigned him a number according to his required priority of care. She then wrote this number in indelible ink on the patient's forehead or, in the event that the forehead was not appropriate, the next available and easily visible piece of healthy skin. This number clearly communicated to the stretcher-bearers where in the hospital the patient was to be taken. No discussion was necessary.

Within moments of arriving, each and every casualty was in the care of a team of highly qualified and trained professionals, appropriate to their most pressing clinical needs. It was the largest and most complex mass casualty situation in which I was ever involved, and yet it was by far the calmest and the most effective. The process was simple, was abundantly clear, and worked with incredible efficiency. We had rehearsed the procedure, prior to deployment during our mission rehearsal exercise in The Netherlands, and I will be forever appreciative for the time, money and effort expended by the ADF to enable us to do that.

The operating theatre swung into action and those patients requiring surgery were triaged once more to establish the order in which they would be treated. The ICU team prepared to receive the first patient from theatre and the hospital hummed with efficiency throughout the night as each patient received care and was allocated a ward bed. As Duty Officer I was working alongside the CO and the Clinical Director to oversee the overall functioning of the hospital throughout the night. I became the primary liaison for the Australian casualties, providing updates to Headquarters and to the immediate chain of command of those within our care. I walked briskly, not quite a run, to fetch blood products and supplies. I ensured that the team were fed and hydrated and I nagged them to rest whenever a moment presented itself. I shuffled and allocated beds, ensuring that the soldiers remained in each other's company wherever possible.

Sadly, one soldier was unconscious in ICU and others had required treatment at the American FST, but I sensed that where possible, they needed to remain together, for now at least. I had listened to the camaraderie that they brought with them from the battlefield, the stories of survival, such incredible and unimaginable stories of survival. I was witness to what I can only describe as an informal and unplanned debrief of a near-death experience among a group of men that no psychologist could ever hope to emulate in any post-critical incident debriefing. They had each experienced the battle in their own way and from their own specific location and perspective and, after it all, they seemed to need to check their stories against those of their comrades, as if trying to piece it all together in their minds. Amazingly, this was occurring in the emergency room and would continue during the night, resuming again in the morning, only to be replayed with equal vigour when their uninjured comrades eventually arrived to visit.

Throughout the candour there was a stark periodic lull in their enthusiastic storytelling that was tinged with the sadness of regret and remorse. Someone had been lost — a female. The only casualty of whom we were aware was an American soldier, who was definitely male. I was confused. Then there were the repeated comments directed at one Australian soldier in particular:

'I'm sorry about Sarbi, mate,' they would say. 'I'm sure they'll find her.' The palpable sorrow among them when 'Sarbi' was mentioned was gut-wrenching, and I didn't even know who they were talking about. I had to be certain that we had accounted for everyone. Perhaps Sarbi was being treated at the American FST? Had I missed something? I enquired gently, yet as directly as possible, 'I'm sorry, but who is Sarbi?'

My heart broke as I stood and listened to the response and felt the mood of the room sink. Sarbi was the explosives detection dog that had been an important member of the operation that day. At some point during the firefight, she and her handler were blown to the ground by a rocket-propelled grenade, severing her leash. Disoriented, she became separated from the convoy and despite her handler's desperate attempts to call her back, she just couldn't catch up to them again. She was last seen running somewhere behind the convoy and was eventually lost from sight. Someone very important to them all had indeed been left behind. I fought back the tears as I thought of my own beautiful dog back in Australia. What would become of Sarbi in this country that had shown it could be so cruel to humans? How could they go home without her?

As the first theatre patient was transferred to ICU, and each of the remaining patients was stabilized and prepared for theatre, my responsibilities settled once more and I sought the clinical comfort of the operating theatre and eventually set to work in the recovery room. I distinctly recall one case that among all the others gave the eventful evening some perspective for me. He was a battle-weary Australian soldier, who I knew from the adrenaline-fuelled anecdotes of the trauma room had on that day fought against other men to preserve the life of his mates alongside him and to save the father, the husband and brother within himself. He was tired. He was dirty. He was broken to such an extent that he would not return to the battlefield before first returning home. As his anaesthetic wore off, he opened his eyes. He looked at me, and with the courtesy of a true gentleman, a tempered soldier, he said three words, 'Thank you, Ma'am.'

When the dust had settled the next day, our first order of business was to retrieve those Australian casualties that had spent the night at the American FST, and finally we would have them all together again to begin preparations for their repatriation to Australia. The morning news informed us that we had received the largest number of Australian combat casualties in one attack since 1971 during the Vietnam War. No wonder we had had such an eventful night! It certainly wasn't important at the time, but with everyone out of immediate danger it gave us cause to reflect upon what we had achieved.

I was not at all surprised that the team, both Australian and Dutch, had done such a magnificent job and, although I know that having Aussies come through the trauma doors had tugged at their heart strings, they had conducted themselves with the utmost professionalism, compassion and good old Aussie mateship. Although on most occasions I struggle to put names to faces, I made a concerted effort to remember the first names of each of the soldiers as we treated them so that when I spoke to their mates and commanders throughout the night I could attempt to convey that they were important to us. To my surprise, I even managed to get a few nicknames memorized.

The soldier who had spent the night in ICU was airlifted out of Tarin Kot to the hospital at Kandahar. I could see that his condition and his departure had an impact on his mates who remained and who had asked to be brought out to see him go. Some of the junior nurses were horrified by what appeared to be the parading of their patient — definitely not something that you would see in a civilian hospital. I began to feel like the old matron of the group as I explained that the bond shared between these men was unique and somehow closer than that of family.

He was their brother, and less than 24 hours ago they had to rely on each other to survive. I speculated that these men were likely to be feeling a range of emotions about his injuries and whether they would ever see him again. I had wrestled with survivor guilt but I had never been in battle nor fought against another human being for my life. I had no right to assume that I knew of anything that they might be feeling, but their request to see their mate before he left was completely reasonable to me and was now also very reasonable to the others in the team.

The ICU team had begun a practice where they would write a message of support for their patients who, due to their critical state, would probably never pass through their care again. This patient was definitely no exception but there was a chance that by virtue of being members of the ADF they might meet him again one day. I was proud of them and this simple act of compassion. They wrote him a card in which they introduced themselves and wished him well in his recovery, and placed it with the personal effects that would accompany him home.

We were not aware of the Battle of Ana Kalay by name, but with the passage of time it would become historic for a number of reasons. These reasons we would discover along with the rest of Australia but we could link them back to that night in Tarin Kot. For their actions, a number of the personnel involved in the battle received awards for gallantry, and Trooper Mark Donaldson was awarded the first Australian Victoria Cross (VC) — our nation's highest award for valour — in 40 years. Then, eighteen months after the battle, explosive detection dog Sarbi was found in Afghanistan by an American soldier who recognized her as not being the usual mongrel mutt a farmer would have. A few words of command in English and this anonymous American GI apparently purchased her from the farmer. Knowing the Aussies were missing an explosives detection dog, he ensured she was returned to Tarin Kot and later back to Australia to be reunited with her handler.

The Air Force Health 'good news story' that would come out of the Battle of Ana Kalay had almost no mention of the work of AUSMTF2. The newly certified C–17 Globemaster capability successfully conducted its first AME out of the Middle East in response to the casualties of the battle. It was a notably impressive milestone for the Air Force with the AME being a testament to much hard work done by Health Services Wing and by Air Lift Group who operated it. I was definitely proud of my colleagues and thrilled with the new AME capability. The C–17 was not yet certified to land in Tarin Kot so the casualties were transported via C–130 to an airfield outside of Afghanistan, where they were then transferred to the C–17 for transport home.

As with the grenade injury to the NATO soldier weeks before, Wing Commander David Scott treated some of the Australian casualties in Tarin Kot with peripheral nerve block infusions to provide them with continuous pain relief for their long journey home. Because of this procedure and its unusual clinical needs and, as he was due to leave Tarin Kot in a few days' time anyway, it made sense that he accompanied the patients home as an adjunct to the AME team, ensuring that the casualties' flight home was pain free.

I had never before seen such proficient use of regional anaesthesia in the field and I came to appreciate the incredible effect that this particular type of pain relief had on the wellbeing of trauma victims and those who cared for them — personally and professionally. As I had suffered severe pain as a result of trauma in the field and during a subsequent AME in East Timor, I appreciated the adverse and compounding effect of pain on the lasting memories associated with my trauma, but also on the experience of my friends and colleagues who witnessed me in such pain.

My observations of trauma victims in Tarin Kot who had their pain completely anaesthetized were that they were more alert and more mobile and able to assist in their own care. Remarkably, though, they were also better able to talk to their comrades and so were able to begin that very early and valuable debrief of their experience, something that may otherwise have had to wait until they were reunited weeks or even months later back in Australia. The soldiers who remained behind told us of how much they appreciated the opportunity to talk to their injured mates, but also of how witnessing the care that they had received provided them with the confidence to put the trauma of battle behind them and go back out beyond the wire once more.

Our Critical Care Team consisted of:

SQNLDR Sharon Cooper (Bown), Officer-in-Charge/Perioperative RN

WGCDR Annette Holian, Orthopaedic Surgeon (Team 1)

SQNLDR Mary Langcake, General Surgeon (Team 1)

WGCDR David Scott, Anaesthetist/Intensivist (Team 1)

WGCDR Gregor Bruce, Orthopaedic Surgeon (Team 2)

SQNLDR Bruce Ashford, General Surgeon (Team 2)

SQNLDR Alexander Donald, Anaesthetist/Intensivist (Team 2)

FLTLT Leslie Lee, Perioperative RN

FLTLT Heather Dodd, Perioperative RN

CPL Rachelle Kucinskis, Advanced Medical Assistant — Perioperative

FLTLT Leigh Twist, 2IC/Intensive Care RN

FLTLT Kelli Mitchener, Intensive Care RN

CPL Sara O'Rourke, Advanced Medical Assistant — ICU.

In my role as OIC, I actively sought recognition for individuals within my team and for the team as a whole. I acknowledged that having been their commander and having shared such intense experiences with them, I may not have been entirely capable of being objective about their performance. Other deployments in recent times had seen far greater casualty numbers than we had. But we were a single team, as close to the frontline as a Critical Care Team could be and we had absolutely no reprieve from the workload, unlike other medical teams. I was intensely proud of each and every one of my team and I applauded their courage in confronting the challenges of this deployment with dignity and pride.

Unofficially, I was informed that there had been so many instances of exceptional and honourable service by ADF members during our period of deployment, that it was unfortunate for our team. I didn't understand what that meant, but then I learned of the quota system applied to Australian Honours and Awards. I absolutely did not wish to deny anyone receiving the recognition they deserved. I was privileged to see the human side of their efforts, and I knew of acts of bravery in battle that far exceeded those of my team, but still I discounted that anyone could believe there can be a quota applied to the number of personnel who will go above and beyond in the service of their country in any particular time period.

The Dutch Commanding Officer, Captain Gemma Flink-Coenen, was much more successful in ensuring that AUSMTF2 was recognized for its performance and its support of ISAF Task Force Uruzgan, with each member awarded the Dutch Commemorative Medal (Peace Operations). This is an award usually given to Dutch servicemen and women only. But somehow Captain Flink-Coenen had convinced her higher chain of command and the Dutch Defence Minister that we were as good as Dutch, and deserved the award that would be presented to the hospital team. It was of such significance that the award was presented to AUSMTF2 in Canberra by the Dutch Defence Minister and in the presence of Captain Flink-Coenen.

AUSMTF2 saw out their Afghanistan deployment as planned and while we never again saw the likes of the Battle of Ana Kalay, we continued to witness the trauma of war and that of living in a country at war. The final trauma that we would experience was that of our own departure. Our Dutch team was only halfway through its tour and our duties were now the responsibility of Dutch critical care specialists. To turn our backs on those with whom we had worked so closely for the past three months seemed premature. I was certainly eager to see my family again and to return to the comfort of my Australian life, and yet I felt that I was abandoning my post.

Some months after my return to Australia, I was asked by a journalist, 'If you were given the opportunity, would you return to Afghanistan?' I replied without hesitation, 'If I were told that there was a Herc turning and burning on the tarmac headed to Afghanistan, then I would be on it.' Years later, exactly the same sentiments — almost word for word — were uttered by other ADF members being interviewed for an ABC-TV documentary, so my feelings were not unique. I was completely honest in my answer, yet a few weeks later I listened to a PTSD researcher explain that one of the telltale signs of PTSD was the desire for the individual to return to the place that had been responsible for their trauma. I didn't understand this. I felt that Afghanistan was where I had performed to the greatest of my ability. Where all of my life's knowledge, skills and experience — my study and experience as a nurse and my training as an Air Force Officer — had culminated in enabling me to deliver care to others and to provide the necessary command and management of my team. I didn't think that it was dysfunctional to want to continue to be of such value.

It took me some time and effort to wind down and fully transition out of Afghanistan. I would find myself sitting on the back deck at home with a glass of red, calculating what time it was in Tarin Kot, wondering who was on roster in which areas of the hospital and wondering where my Australian team were now and what they were doing. I was fortunate that as a military nurse I recognized my hypervigilance and I knew that I had to find a way to come back home and resume a more realistic pace of living. Sure I had to be hypervigilant in Afghanistan but to do so back home would slowly kill me.

I found a yoga teacher in Townsville whose amazing efforts helped me transition from warzone operative to something more akin to a peace-loving hippy. It amused my friends and family but it saved me. I would never again be able to look at red meat without seeing the tattered flesh of young men and so I also became a vegetarian. My yoga teacher told me red meat was bad for my joints and Conway told me it was bad for our budget, so I never felt too sorry about the change in diet.

The dust of Uruzgan is indeed pervasive and it is not easily shaken off. It is already buried beneath Australian soil within the remains of those who, in her service, have paid the ultimate sacrifice of war, and it certainly threatens to cloak and clog the minds of a generation of Australian service personnel. Yet I value the time I spent there. My operational service in places such as Afghanistan has allowed me to accomplish the goal that I had set out to achieve when I decided to join the Air Force almost a decade earlier. I have certainly felt the full depth of reality of life with an intensity that cannot easily be denied and for that I am more fortunate than many.

CHAPTER 11
THE DARKNESS

No, that's not adrenaline, neither is that one. Frantically shuffling through the drug ampoules I couldn't find the only chance that this Australian soldier had of surviving this flight.

'Sharon, where's the adrenaline?' the doctor screeched impatiently.

There it was. With fumbling hands I had drawn it up and, glancing toward the patient, I saw that he was conscious and gazing around the aircraft. Twisty was at his side. All was calm and peaceful as if the cardiac arrest moments earlier had been a figment of my imagination. Twisty and I chatted casually. Her partner was flying the C-130 Hercules transport today and despite the momentary chaos of our one and only patient dying for a brief period, all was well. Then the aircraft took a surprising and steep turn.

As always for me nowadays, a sudden move in the air breeds anxiety and I could feel my heart racing as I reached for my seat. Twisty was thrown off balance and our shared gaze communicated, 'What the hell was that?' The expected levelling of the wings did not occur. The aircraft plunged into a steep dive — I could see the ground and the trees through the window. We were surely going in. I threw myself backward into a very plush seat, unusual for a Herc, but something to ponder if and when I survived this.

'Twisty! Put your seatbelt on!' I screamed as I grabbed for mine, fearing that I would not have time to secure myself before impact. My heart raced and I once again knew that all too familiar fear that had haunted me since the last crash. Why me? Not again. My heart ached for not being able to save Twisty from the horrors of my experience.

'Twisty! Put your seatbelt on!' I screamed it over and over and over as I watched her stumble around the cabin knowing that with each passing second she was never going to be able to secure herself — she was not going to have a chance to save herself. My fear intensified as I wondered where we might be. Had we crossed the border yet? Were we about to crash in Afghanistan and find ourselves at the mercy of a ruthless enemy? The Taliban didn't care who I was; they just saw me as a westerner and I would pay dearly for my country of birth and for my choice of career.

I sat bolt upright in bed, heart pounding, my skin lathered in cold sweat. Fear gripped my mind. With the realization that I was safely in my bed at home, I could once again shake off the attack, only for it to be replaced by frustration and a sense of tedium.

'Damn!' I muttered, knowing that to drift back to sleep would take me right back into that doomed aircraft. It was 6.30 a.m. on a Saturday morning, a time reserved specifically for a luxurious sleep in, yet I knew that there would not be any more peaceful sleep for me this morning.

The nightmares were rare these days and not nearly as prevalent as they had been in the early years following the crash. As I prepared my breakfast I pondered the newest aspect to my crash nightmare. Did I still feel a need to care for the members of AUSMTF2? Did I carry a fear of capture from my Afghanistan experience? Was I terrorized by having witnessed firsthand what the Taliban was prepared to do to a human body? I knew I had met elements of their fold, and had touched the terror and grotesque trauma they had inflicted upon humans and humanity. I resented that they had had such an impact upon me. I had learned the immense value of human life and I had witnessed the devotion to humanity displayed by individuals who would sacrifice everything for strangers, and for what they believed to be the greater good. The perfectly rational human fear that I felt as a result of my interactions with them was what I believed set me apart from them. I understood the pain of life-altering trauma and as a result I would never wish it upon any other being, let alone inflict it.

When I returned from Afghanistan I resumed my role as Officer-in-Charge of No. 1 Expeditionary Health Squadron — Detachment Townsville, where I remained until January 2011. My time in Afghanistan and the people with whom I had served had taught me a great deal about leadership, and about the importance of preparing me and my ADF health colleagues for our primary role of providing combat health support. Once again, my experience of operational deployment had reinvigorated my passion for Air Force nursing and for the continuing need to advocate for the health and welfare of ADF members and their families.

Afghanistan had given me a greater appreciation for the service and sacrifices made by veterans of war. Not just the soldiers in ground combat but the aircrew who flew in some of the most dangerous conditions in the world and the personnel by whom they were supported, and the sailors who spent months at sea, often far from the so-called glory of the battlefield, but equally as vital to the mission in their role. My relationship with those for whom I was responsible to provide healthcare had changed. I now had a more useful understanding of the levels of fitness and health required of certain roles and, sadly, I had also gained valuable insight into the horrors that our men and women had been witnessing overseas. While I had always been eager to deploy, my garrison support role in Australia now took on new meaning.

Away from work, Conway and I were married in 2009 and two years later we welcomed the arrival of a beautiful baby boy. I farewelled my team at No. 1 Expeditionary Health Squadron — Detachment Townsville and enjoyed a twelve-month period of maternity leave as I turned my focus to my newest role of motherhood. Returning to work in 2012, I took my passion for Air Force nursing and combat health support into a new project management role in which I contributed to the re-organization of Air Force nursing. I appreciated the opportunity and was proud of the accomplishments of the project, but I began to feel distant from the reality of the operational role of an Air Force Nursing Officer.

I don't recall exactly when, but after a series of medical assessments conducted by three independent psychiatrists appointed by the Department of Veterans' Affairs, I was diagnosed with post-traumatic stress disorder, PTSD. My symptoms included recurring nightmares, intrusive thoughts and flashbacks related to my helicopter crash, fear of flying, hypervigilance in the presence of aircraft — whether I was in them, close to them on the ground or simply within earshot of them — and actively avoiding people and activities that reminded me of the crash.

I denied my diagnosis, arguing that my symptoms were a perfectly rational or indeed a normal reaction to an abnormal experience. I now had a memory of what happens when an aircraft crashes and when you experience acute pain. I am afraid to fly. I am afraid for my husband and my children to fly. My PTSD was about fear, the fear of being afraid. I had been through two near-death experiences in a short period. My near-death experience following surgery to repair my fractured jaw was peaceful, it was also a little confusing, but ultimately it was a calm experience of drifting off to sleep. Conversely, my near-death experience in a helicopter crash was the most intense emotion that I had ever known. I expected to die; I expected to experience unimaginable pain. As a result, I learned to fear ever experiencing that fear or that level of pain again.

I believed that my fear and avoidance behaviours were simply learned acts of survival. In a way, the Department of Veterans' Affairs agreed. They accepted that I suffered with PTSD, but not to a level that warranted financial compensation. That was fine by me. I didn't want financial compensation, but nor did I want to be labelled with PTSD. My diagnosis caused me to resent the chronic pain and the sleep deprivation of my spinal injury. If not for their constant and inescapable reminder of the crash, my mind may have been better able to heal and to forget. They prevented me from ever truly leaving my experience behind, and hence my PTSD persisted.

Despite my own rational explanation of my symptoms I was nevertheless deeply ashamed of my diagnosis so I simply denied it. I did not disclose it to anyone other than Conway and my treating healthcare team. Even uttering the words to them left me feeling weak. Awareness of PTSD within the ADF was increasing, but from my perspective that appeared to be occurring largely within Army, where PTSD rates seemed to be much higher.

The stigma surrounding PTSD, or simply the ignorance demonstrated by some individuals towards the condition, became directly apparent to me from the comments and opinions of my own colleagues — fellow Air Force Officers who were unaware of my diagnosis and obviously unable to link a life-threatening event such as a helicopter crash with the development of PTSD. There was a young Medical Officer who, never having been deployed, declared that 'those with a diagnosis of PTSD should never be deployed'. I understood the clinical context of his reasoning, assuming that he was referring to the increased risk of PTSD developing with subsequent exposure to trauma, but he didn't choose to include any evidence-based clinical reasoning in his very public assertion.

Much later in my career there was a fellow Senior Officer who, during a conversation about PTSD, challenged me with, 'You can't tell me that you don't have PTSD!' I was stunned by such a forthright accusation regarding something so personal, and yet I have never been one to lie so I felt no choice but to respond.

'Of course, I bloody well do. I rode a helicopter into the ground and now I'm afraid to fly! No surprises there really!'

Some may scoff and dismiss my perception of having experienced the stigma associated with mental health as a result of me being hypersensitive. They're right. I was ashamed of my diagnosis and of what I perceived to be my weakness. This made me incredibly sensitive to the views of others. But, ultimately, that is exactly what stigma is — a mark of social disgrace that would set me apart from my peers.

My fear of being found out pushed me to challenge my symptoms head on. I flew despite the fear. Unbeknown to me, I was engaging in my own personal style of exposure therapy. I didn't obsessively seek out opportunities to expose myself to flying nor deliberately make myself uncomfortable, but I doggedly refused to back away from my fear. I would never suggest that an individual's personal battle with PTSD can be overcome so simply. My PTSD was of the lowest possible level recognizable by the Department of Veterans' Affairs. This is in stark contrast to those whose lives are paralyzed by their PTSD and the far too many who feel driven to end their lives as a result. But my service to my country had changed me and it became important for me to understand and to accept that change. If I could not, then how could I expect the social stigma created by the views of others to change. Why was it so difficult to find peace, when the sacrifice made was in the service of the nation?

The men and women of the ADF provide a unique capability to the government of Australia. No matter an election outcome, the 24-hour news cycle, or the acknowledgement that the debt that our country owes us can never be repaid, the men and women of the ADF will always serve the government of the day in defending and securing our national interests. The capability is often one of diplomacy and of posturing, but historically, presently and possibly for perpetuity, it is also one of combat.

With this capability comes great risk and great sacrifice, and quite simply that is the nature of the job. Individuals involved in high-risk activities will by the very nature of those activities risk injury and death. In black and white it makes perfect sense. Yet, in my experience it is a fact that is politically and socially painful to acknowledge. The personnel of the ADF do a dangerous job as safely as possible, but that does not negate the fact that they do a dangerous job. So many people are shocked to hear of my service-related injuries and the fact that they were sustained by a nurse in a helicopter crash in a foreign country.

I chose to be where I was at that moment in time, and a series of personal choices led me to that crash site: I chose to join the military; I chose to deploy to an impoverished nation to provide assistance; I chose to board a helicopter in that country and I even chose the seat that I would occupy that day. Unfortunately, I came to realize the risks of the choices that I had made. Resolving to accept responsibility for my choices and, thus my injuries, helped me to make peace with the sacrifices I had made. Equally, so did the expression of gratitude by others for my service.

In the days following the crash, I felt the warm embrace of the care and concern of so many, including my Commanding Officer, Chief of the Defence Force and Chief of the Air Force. Their heartfelt concern inspired me to get back on my feet and back on with my life. But there were also direct expressions of gratitude that provided me with a similar sense of peace and resilience: the stranger in the street who acknowledged my uniform and took the time to thank me for my service; the ever-increasing numbers of Australians who honour ANZAC Day; those who recognized my career achievements as more substantial than my involvement in a helicopter crash; and the increased emphasis placed on contemporary service at the Australian War Memorial — a place in which I always feel as if I have returned home.

Of most significance, though, must be the acknowledgement of the risks of service, and the absolute and unfaltering knowledge and confidence that, when ADF members are injured or killed, that they and their families will be taken into the arms of the country for which they served, to be forever valued and cared for. There could be no greater expression of value or gratitude, yet it is in this area that many veterans feel let down.

In my experience, having been 'broken' has provided me with an opportunity for growth, an opportunity to be even more complete than I was before. Being challenged by loss, damage, disfigurement and disability, my potential to rebuild and to overcome was revealed. It revealed a capability within me that I would not have otherwise known I possessed — a part of myself that could have only ever been revealed by first cracking the outer shell. The person that I was before I was injured and the one I sometimes still long for, was only ever a superficial version of the real me, providing mere glimpses of my true potential. It has only been through the loss and the suffering I have endured that I have been challenged to truly explore the extent of my capabilities.

It has taken severe trauma and damage to reveal my depths. Such a realization brings with it a fear that there may indeed still be far greater challenges waiting for me to reveal far greater depths. I hesitate to imagine what they may be but I know that in reality I have not even begun to experience loss. I still have the love and presence of my husband and my children. I still have life, and I have only ever faced death as an imminent possibility within the context of my near-death experiences and not as a prolonged certainty associated with a terminal diagnosis, such as that suffered by my mother.

Will I now face loss and death as an opportunity for growth? I think not. I have not yet mastered the skill of equanimity such that I can easily ride out the rollercoaster of emotion of our human existence. I do however hold on to the deep-seated personal drive that emerged within those early days following my crash, the vow to be a survivor of my circumstances and never a victim.

CHAPTER 12

THE DAWN

I was privileged and deeply honoured to be invited to contribute to the Australian War Memorial's 2014 National ANZAC Day Dawn Service through co-presenting the pre-dawn address alongside Lieutenant Commander Desmond Woods. Dr Brendan Nelson, now Director of the Australian War Memorial, had requested that I provide an insight into the contemporary service of the ADF. I had two options to consider in achieving his aim: I could either read a series of extracts from the diaries of ADF personnel who had served since the cessation of the Second World War, or I could choose to write a personal account of my own service.

I questioned why, in a generation that had produced four recipients of Australia's Victoria Cross, my contribution would be relevant. Dr Nelson informed me that Corporal Ben Roberts-Smith VC, MG, would deliver the Dawn Service address, and that I would provide a contemporary voice for Air Force and for women. More significantly, though, he believed that I had something to say that Australia needed to hear.

On 25 April 2014, I left Conway in a Canberra hotel room with our sons, three-year-old Ty and four-week-old Austin, to front a crowd of 37,000 people, including the unexpected appearance of Prince William and his wife, Catherine, Duchess of Cambridge. Nervously I mounted the podium and gazed out into the darkness. In the dim pre–dawn light I saw thousands of faces now looking up at me. This is what I said:

As we stand here together, awaiting the dawn, the shadow of night tenderly cloaks each of us in a comforting sanctuary of darkness.

In the early hours before the dawn, we are drawn from our private homes to gather here as a community of ordinary strangers, united by the actions of extraordinary strangers who fought for their country, their mates, and their lives, 99 years ago upon the shores of Gallipoli.

They were the soldiers of Australia and New Zealand. They were the ANZACs.

The darkness before the dawn clutches us. We are unable to see that which lies beyond the light; unable to perceive that which may bring us harm. Our security, once delivered by extraordinary strangers of yesterday, remains safely entrusted and protected by the extraordinary strangers of today: the men and women of the Australian Defence Force; men and women who will give their all to defend you and to ensure that you may forever gather here within the comfort of their ever-watchful shadow.

As the ANZACs approached the shores of Gallipoli in the early hours before the dawn, the shadow of darkness may have shielded their presence from the enemy, yet in turn, it also shielded from them the treacherous peril that lay in wait. From the ANZACs to Afghanistan, the shadow of night that offered protection equally exposed their vulnerability.

Even I, a Nursing Officer of the Royal Australian Air Force, have lived in such a place: where both security and vulnerability arrive with the

*darkness of nightfall, where we deliberately ensure that all light is ex-
tinguished to remove us from the view of those that would do us harm,
those that lie and wait for their black cloak of darkness to descend.*

*I have watched from the dirt ramparts of the base at Tarin Kot while
brave men and women left the warm glow of its lights to slip silently
into the cold clutches of the night beyond, and put themselves in harm's
way to protect us. I have felt their departure as they slip into the invisi-
bility of that very darkness in the company of their comrades, striving to
shield you from the world's unimaginable shadows.*

*I have heard the noise of battle in the distance, taken the radio call and
annotated the Nine Liner, and then eagerly awaited the sound of rotor
blades that would deliver the war to me.*

*I have awaited their return and tended their wounds, never able to
fully comprehend the darkness of man that they encountered upon their
journey. I have witnessed their adrenaline-fuelled highs of survival and
their immense depths of despair at the loss of a mate. I have laughed
reservedly at the often black-humoured stories of soldiers who photo-
graph their legs before a patrol, just in case they never saw them again,
and faced the reality of their need to loosely wear a tourniquet on each
limb, ready to stem the almost inevitable haemorrhage that could end
their life. I have been privileged to hear of unimaginable acts of bravery
and self-preservation, and I have stood by silently to attempt to pick up
the pieces when it all falls apart.*

I have worn their blood.

So many of us have worn their blood.

I have seen the strongest and finest reduced to flesh, and witnessed the death of innocence and a once supposed sense of immortality.

I have stood in a trauma room surrounded by the victims of an IED blast and watched as our finest doctors, nurses and medics ask themselves not just 'which casualty first?' but 'which wound on which casualty first?' I have marvelled at their skill, their courage, their resilience. Together, we have waded through their blood, fighting our own battle to protect and secure. Fending off the enemy of death, of disfigurement, of disability; tapping into that unique fighting spirit of the Australian soldier before us, whose courage and sheer determination will see them through another day.

I have sat in silent contemplation among peers as we reflect upon decisions made, lives saved and lives lost as a result of, and in spite of our efforts.

I have seen them arrive at the edge of the battlefield and known that when they departed for home, that they would never again be the same. I have gathered the passports of Australian soldiers who were to be repatriated back to Australia, and not been able to match the battle weary faces to the documents in my hands.

I have always, always hoped that they will forever find the strength and courage to emerge from the too often persistent shadows, to stand tall in the world for which they have given so much to secure, to stand shoulder to shoulder with comrades, loved ones and ordinary strangers in these early hours before the dawn. I have always hoped that they would somehow come to value and accept that which they have seen, that which they have done and, mostly, that which they have given. I have hoped that they will see the advances and not just the retreats, the gains and not just the losses and, ultimately, the immense value of their service. I have clung to the revelry of their joyous reunion, their unique bond of brotherhood, of victory, of realizing the reality of just what they would and could do to protect each other. I have trusted that this will help them to emerge from the shadows and once again feel the sun upon their faces.

I have held their widows and widowers, consoled their parents, their brothers, sisters, and friends, and gazed upon their children, some too young to comprehend the enormity of that which they have lost.

I have crawled out of the darkness and I have fought for my life.

I am no different from many other Australians. So many of those like me, stand silently among you today; each of them once more shielded by the darkness, each of them withholding the horrors of war, still endeavouring to provide protection to each and every one of you.

They will not likely share the truth of their experience. They will not likely ever find the words to do it justice and, even if they could, it is not likely that anyone other than the brothers and sisters that stood alongside them could ever come close to understanding.

They will mostly choose the anonymity of the darkness before the dawn, the anonymity of the dark suit before the uniform.

Shining upon the walls of the Memorial behind me are the names and faces of the 40 soldiers killed in Afghanistan — Australia's longest and most recent war; brave men who paid the ultimate sacrifice in the service of their country.

You do not see the 261 who were wounded.

You do not see those who wrestle with post-traumatic stress disorder, or the other mental health issues that have resulted from their service.

You do not see the 26,500 who, if asked, will claim to have simply served.

You may not hear their voices as they reflect: 'If I had died over there, I would have been remembered forever, but I survived and my name will never be known.'

They stand silently among you today.

As the dawn delivers the daylight, pause to reflect upon the memory of those that have gone before us in your name, those whose faces and names grace the walls of our Memorial. But, I implore of you to also pause and watch carefully as the dawn sheds light upon the faces of the extraordinary strangers that stand beside you. Contemplate, if only for a moment, that which they may have done, that which they may willingly continue to do, so that you may return to stand here each year, in the darkness before the dawn awaiting the light of a new day and the warmth of the sun, a community of ordinary strangers . . . drawn together to honour their extraordinary service.

Lest we forget.

As I turned my back on the podium and the assembled crowd, I looked up at the majestic stone walls of the Australian War Memorial, standing as it always had as silent witness to the sacrifices of our country. I looked into the eyes of an Australian soldier whose image had been projected upon the surface of the Memorial in honour of his memory and of the sacrifice of his life in Afghanistan. My physical pain was acute that morning. I knew that I had pushed hard against the boundaries of my tolerance to be here. I had given birth only four weeks earlier, had flown all the way from Townsville, and was now standing in the chill of the early morning Canberra air and my back was punishing me for my hubris.

I had fought my way back into service many times since that fateful day in June 2004, but instinct told me that this time the outcome would be different. I had not given my life for my country but I had, like so many others, given enough that my life would never be the same for having done so.

With a nod to the ghostly image before me, I acknowledged that I was walking away from what may be my final act of service. I would never again wear the uniform of the ADF, a uniform in which we had both served, but for which he had ultimately died. My mission was over.

EPILOGUE

On 7 September 2015, I was discharged from the Royal Australian Air Force, having been deemed medically unfit to continue to serve. I was not surprised by the decision of the Central Medical Review Board, as I had requested that I be afforded the dignity of a clear and final decision in preference to a protracted and painful conflict. And while I was not surprised by the outcome, I still felt gutted. As I read through the letter advising me of the Board's final determination, I felt that I was learning of the death of someone dear to me. I had joined the ADF to serve my country, for which I felt an immense sense of pride, and now I had to attempt to accept that serving my country no longer served me or my family. For that, I felt the most intense sense of shame.

For eleven years I had pushed myself to continue to meet the employment requirements of military service, particularly the physical fitness requirements. Having done so, I had accelerated the degradation of my spinal injury and the intensity of my pain. This led to a pain-induced intolerance of others and sleep deprivation. The changes within me that had resulted from my service had reached a limit that prevented me from continuing to serve, but they had also reached my self-imposed limit of who I was prepared to become.

I had loved my job. My identity as an operational Air Force Nurse was one with which I connected more strongly than any other in my life. It constantly challenged me — professionally, physically, psychologically and spiritually; in doing so, it had revealed a part of me that I would never have otherwise realized. It lifted me up and satisfied my ego more than any other identity that I had. While I strived to fulfil the roles and responsibilities of my positions, there was always that nagging depletion in my ability to meet the basic requirements of employment. I had learned from experiencing the loss of my colleagues in the Sea King crash on the Indonesian island of Nias that I could never again send others into operational service if I was not fit or prepared to go myself.

I began to grieve for the young Tasmanian nurse standing at RAAF Base Williams (Point Cook) on the edge of Australia's oldest military airfield, and upon the precipice of a life-changing career. I didn't grieve for her to return, but I missed her innocence and her wide-eyed enthusiasm for adventure. If I could stand beside her and whisper in her ear, I would not tell her to step back from the verge of my life. I would tell her to strive forward with pride and to hold fast to her values and ambition to make the world a better place, for her simply having been in it. I would tell her of the amazing opportunities that lay before her and of the people that she would meet who would both enrich and fortify her being. I would tell her that there would be sacrifices, but in making those sacrifices she would not lose anything, she would merely pass something wonderful on to someone else. In losing her health and fitness she would save the mother of children in an impoverished land; in losing time with her loved ones, she would give time in the service of others.

I would tell her that she would become the collateral damage of the ADF's mission to defend Australia and its interests, but that the unintentional loss that she would suffer would be of tremendous personal value to her and to many others. To reach the stars, she would endure adversity, but the value of both the journey and the destination would be worthwhile.

ABBREVIATIONS, ACRONYMS AND TERMINOLOGY

1 ATHS	No. 1 Air Transportable Health Squadron, RAAF
1 EHS	No. 1 Expeditionary Health Squadron, RAAF
1 FD HOSP	1st Field Hospital, Australian Army (known as 'First Field')
3 HOSP	No. 3 RAAF Hospital (known as 'Three Hospital')
6 HOSP	No. 6 RAAF Hospital (known as 'Six Hospital')
ADC	Aide-de-Camp
ADF	Australian Defence Force
AEOO	Aeromedical Evacuation Operations Officer
AME	Aeromedical Evacuation
ANA	Afghan National Army
ANP	Afghan National Police
ANZAC	Australia and New Zealand Army Corps of WWI or a member thereof
ASF	Aeromedical Staging Facility

AUSMTF2	Australian Medical Task Force 2
Bushmaster PMV	An Australian armoured vehicle (Protected Mobility Vehicle)
C-17	Lockheed C-17 Globemaster jet transport aircraft
C-130	Lockheed C-130 Hercules (Herc) turboprop transport aircraft
CAF	Chief of Air Force
CASEVAC	Casualty Evacuation — the extraction of a wounded person
CASG	Comoro Airfield (Dili Airport) Support Group
CCT	Critical Care Team consisting of surgeons and intensive care specialists
CO	Commanding Officer (In RAAF terms, a Commander of a Squadron; In Army terms, a Commander of a unit-sized element such as a battalion or a regiment)
CSSD	Central Sterile Supply Department
DCO	Defence Community Organisation
DEO	Direct Entry Officer
DET	Detachment
Digger	The nickname for an Australian Army soldier
DS	Directing Staff
Dustoff	The callsign, and nickname, of a US Army Aeromedical Evacuation helicopter
DVA	Department of Veterans' Affairs
EMS	Emergency Medical Service
F88	AUSteyr automatic assault rifle (Australian designation for the Steyr AUG)
FAST	Fly Away Surgical Team

FOB/FSB	Forward Operating Base/Fire Support Base
FST	Forward Surgical Team — usually at a Role 1 Medical Facility
Gat	Euphemism for a gun, in particular a rifle. From 'Gatling gun', a crank-handle operated multi-barrel weapon from 19th-century United States.
Hesco	Trade name for a pre-fabricated defensive wall system using large bags containing earth
HSW	Health Services Wing
HUMVEE	US armoured vehicle (HMMWV High Mobility Multipurpose Wheeled Vehicle)
ICU	Intensive Care Unit
IED	Improvised Explosive Device
INTERFET	International Force East Timor
LN	Local National (a civilian from the host country)
MINDEF	Minister for Defence
Nine Liner	A standardized format for the request for a CASEVAC consisting of nine lines of information including location, patient's condition, enemy action, etc.
MEDASST	Medical Assistant (Medic)
MO	Medical Officer (Doctor)
NO	Nursing Officer (Nurse)
OC	Officer Commanding (RAAF title for a commander of a Wing)
OIC	Officer-in-Command (Generic term for a person who is in command of a sub-unit or detachment)
OTS	Officer Training School (of the RAAF)

Permanent Air Force	Full time Air Force as opposed to Air Force Reserve.
PTSD	Post-traumatic stress disorder
RAAF	Royal Australian Air Force or Air Force
RN	Registered Nurse
Role 2(+) or (E)	Role 2 Enhanced Medical Facility
Role 3	Role 3 Medical Facility
SASR	Special Air Service Regiment — Special Forces unit
SF/Special Forces	Highly trained soldiers specializing in irregular combat
SQNWOFF	Squadron Warrant Officer — the squadron's senior airman Warrant Officer
Tarin Kot (TK)	A large town in Uruzgan that was the site of a major NATO base
Timor Leste	East Timor as spoken in the Tetum language of its inhabitants
UNAMET	United Nations Missions East Timor
UNMILHOSP	UN Military Hospital
Uruzgan	A province of Afghanistan where the bulk of Australia's ground force operations were carried out. Also spelt Oruzgan.

INDEX